Me+You

(Love and Other Various Emotions)

ANNA BOWEN

ANNA BOWEN

CONTENTS

ANNA BOWEN

ACKNOWLEDGMENTS

My everlasting gratitude goes out to everyone who made this book possible. To my friends and family members who were willing to share so much with me. Their courageous struggles towards finding commitment, their compassion for one another, and their conscious choice to love each other every day have made this book a reality.

Love is Patient, love is kind.

It does not envy, it does not boast, it is not proud.

It does not dishonor others, it is not self-seeking, it is not easily

angered, it keeps no record of wrongs.

Love does not delight in evil but rejoices with the truth.

It always protects, always trusts, always hopes, always

perseveres.

--Corinthians 13:4-7--

ANNA BOWEN

JUST THE WAY YOU ARE

Kate, 32

Lamont, 49

married 2 years

Kate and Lamont recently moved to Long Beach where Lamont is attending graduate school to become a teacher. While Lamont is going to school and teaching undergraduate classes, Kate is taking the month off to furnish and set up their new apartment.

Hi. I'm Kate and I'm thirty-two.

I'm Lamont and I'm forty-nine…nine…nine…

He's as old as the hills.

Okay, careful. I'm fragile.

We've been married almost two years. And it's his favorite thing to tell the story of how we met, so I'll let him tell it.

It's not. She likes to think it's my favorite thing. I do enjoy it on occasion but not as a dog and pony, "Let's tell this story for the eight thousandth time."

That's true. I do tend to be like, "Go ahead baby, you love to tell it." So we were both living in New York, traveling to Connecticut, which was about an hour on the metro north train. And you can take the metro north from 42nd street or 125th street. At that time I was living on the Upper East Side and Lamont was living in Harlem, so we both took it from 125th street.

I saw Kate trot by with her fifteen bags and she seemed to know where she was going, so I followed her up to the platform and said, "Excuse me." She said, "Yes?" And she smiled. "Are you going on train number…?" And she said…

"*Yes.*"

"Oh, me too! I'm Lamont."

"*Hi! I'm Kate.*"

I said, "Kate? That name sounds Irish. My ex-girlfriend was Irish. She was crazy."

And I'm thinking, "Oh really? <u>She's</u> crazy? You probably made her crazy." So the train came and I was like, "I'm gonna sit over here." Away from this guy.

She escaped from me is what she did.

With my journal.

Yeah, so me and my Popeye's chicken went to another area to sit.

And I went to write in my journal: "Met a guy on the train platform. <u>Not interested</u>."

Underlined. So then we both got off at the same stop and ran into each other again on the platform. I asked her where she was going and realized it was pretty close to where I was headed, so I asked if she would like to split a cab.

Our driver's name was Ann.

I'm so glad you remember that. So Ann drove us at about the speed of a mule.

Oh my god, we were literally getting passed by tractors. It should've taken about forty-five minutes to get where we were going and I think it took us about two hours. But that's when I discovered Lamont had a sense of humor.

Yes, I was in the back crackin' jokes. Whatever I said it was very catchy. Kate liked it. So I asked for her number before we parted ways.

And I gave it to him.

So that's how we met. When we got back to New York we just started hanging out from time to time. We actually hung out more in groups than one on one at first.

One of the first times we hung out we played strip pool at my friend's apartment. Whenever someone else got the ball in, the other person would have to remove an item of clothing. Then whoever lost had to do a striptease. Lamont was losing and I was a ball away from having him have to do a striptease…and then I shot the eight ball in…so I lost.

But she didn't do the striptease!

Because I'm a lady.

I should've known then, when it comes to competition, she cheats.

It's true. Listen, you were never going to use that "Q" in Scrabble, it didn't matter.

She is not the best sport when it comes to games.

We don't play Scrabble anymore together. It's a bad idea. Scrabble's boring! I'm sorry, I love words and reading and stuff, but Scrabble's boring.

It's only boring when you lose.

No. It's boring when your partner takes three hours to make a word.

Anyway, we started dating. We didn't really take it too seriously, but somehow here we are.

We're stuck. Like a bad penny.

Like a penny with a hole in it!

He met the family within a few months and they all loved him.

Oh yeah, she threw the family on me within six weeks of dating.

He did really well.

Well I do well with women. All the ladies. Except for Grandma.

No, Grandma didn't like him. When I told her his name, she said, "Is he French?" But then she was concerned because he ended up being black instead. She came around eventually.

I thought Kate was kind of cool. I didn't put too much weight in the relationship at first. We were just having a good time, you know? We dated for three years before I proposed. And the proposal takes us back to that train platform. I told her there was a party in Harlem and it was so funny because she was in no mood to go.

Well it was raining cats and dogs, and I had worked all day. But he kept pleading with me, so I put on an outfit begrudgingly.

When we got on the platform, I tried to steer her back to where we first met. I was like, "Oh baby look, that's where we met, I haven't been inside since." And she said, "Aww, I haven't either." So we went inside and reminisced a little bit downstairs, and then went up onto the platform. But there were, like, eight thousand people there so I kept waiting for the train to pull out. Finally a train left and I got on one knee.

Right next to the recycling bins.

I didn't look to see where I was, I just thought to myself, "The coast is clear, let's get it." So I got on one knee and the first thing she said was, "Baby, get up! You're gonna get your pants all wet!" And then, when she realized what I was doing, she turned around and ran the other direction.

I did a little dance and then I came back. He makes it sound like I took off or something. Then I told him to get up...and then I said yes. So we were engaged for a year and then we got married!

The wedding was cool. It was a great day. It was beautiful.

We spent so much time and energy working on it. The ceremony was pretty amazing, I thought.

I don't even know. I cried through three-fourths of it so I don't even know. From the first downbeat of the first song, I was boohooing. I was just so happy to be there.

It was so special. I mean the reception was fun...it was just a big party. But I really felt that the ceremony was this joining together of two halves. And we sensed the profundity of it while we were in it, you know? We managed to create our own thing. We didn't do Bible readings; we read poetry instead. And there was a lot of Gospel, Broadway and Pop music.

It was the ceremony we wanted.

We really created it ourselves. Lamont's nephew is a Baptist minister and my uncle is a Catholic priest so we really brought it all together. One of them did the opening prayer and the other one did the vows. There was never any weirdness between our families even though we come from such different backgrounds.

Yeah, Kate's family is great.

Our families really jumped right in and accepted us as a couple. Although the age difference has been challenging for us. And the race thing…it's never an issue and yet, it's always an issue.

I think the race thing runs deeper than the age thing though. When I was thirty-two, I saw no end to what I was doing. No end whatsoever. I had no other considerations but me, even if I was in a relationship. I only thought about what I wanted and what I could do to get what I wanted. My priorities have changed since then. Now that I am married and I do want kids, the things that used to be important to me aren't important anymore. The thing is, they're still important to Kate. But I don't begrudge her. Whatever she wants to do with her career I'm happy with. Sometimes it feels like she's just getting started. But I know that even if she spreads her wings and flies, she will always come back to me.

Well, Lamont has things that he wants to accomplish in his life and as he gets older he feels like he has less and less time to accomplish them. He wants a family and he wants to settle down. And so do I, but I feel like I have all the time in the world to have those things.

And I don't. It's something we're negotiating as we go along. But as far as the race thing goes: Kate is the first woman (and I've dated a few white girls) that I didn't care if there were sisters walkin' by giving me stank face.

I don't even notice that stuff most of the time.

I don't care because I love Kate that much. That really speaks to me because any other time I would have been so aware of it and anxious about it. I'm still aware of it, but I just don't care.

It comes up in ways that you don't expect. And black people can be just as racist as white people in that regard so you become aware of it from both sides. But we always say, "We are the future!"

When I met Kate's family I was actually very suspicious of them. They were so open and nice to me. I said, "Okay, your family scares me, because they're <u>too</u> nice. And it's genuine. And you feel it."

The race thing has come up, I'd say, when we were choosing a church. I am the product of one tradition and Lamont is the product of another tradition. Both traditions are very important to us because it's how we were raised. It's something we can't help. So that's something we have to figure out. We're a little bit concerned if we're going to raise a biracial child. What schools we want to send them to and what traditions we want them to have and stuff like that. But I have become much more aware of what it's like to be viewed as a minority which is good for me. I mean I'm not a minority obviously.

You're becoming one!

But I've become more aware of things like, "Wow, there are absolutely no other black people here at all…" It's just another awareness. Which is good.

When I was in high school in the late seventies, I had a blond haired, blue-eyed girlfriend that my teachers tried to talk me out of taking to prom. I dealt with things like that. Those types of things, you carry them with you, you know? I'm glad the world is not that way anymore but I also know that it ain't Shangri-La no matter how you shape it.

When people say that we're "post racial" I always want to be like, "Really? What exactly does that mean? Is that just a nice thing to say? Do you mean that we have different approaches to racism or different ways of interpreting racism?" Racism is still there. We're not post racial. But Lamont and I, despite our differences, have the same values. We have the same sense of humor. We have the same attitudes towards family and money and life. And those are the things you really need, more than just being in love. You need a shared sense of values and the same sense of humor, 'cause that's what's going to get you through.

Because it's hard! There's so much insecurity in life. You have to find your strength and your self-esteem. You have to be able to really get a true sense of who you are and find how you fit with this other person.

I think for the first four years, this relationship was my rock. Then it became something to be worked at and maintained. Or "given attention," I should say. And that has been an interesting shift. But it's inevitable. It's the way it is. Ebbs and flows and stuff like that. You need to be able to say to your partner, "I'm being needy right now and I need this from you." And the other person needs to be able to be okay with that.

You have to be secure and have a level of trust so no matter what else is happening, you can say, "Okay, this person has my back. This person is the one." When you don't feel that, it can erode everything.

There are also times when you have to let it go. When you're just dating, you can think to yourself, "Oh, this kind of bothers me…" But when you're married, especially if it's a fundamental personality thing or an upbringing thing…well, that person is going to have that problem for the rest of your lives together. Therefore, the problems that you have seem much more intense than they may or may not be.

There are things that we all bring into a relationship. I won't say "baggage," but it's your "stuff" that you've accumulated over the course of your life. And you have expectations for your life: For your career and for your love…whatever. You have an idea of what you think those things are or what those things should be.

But then you realize that it's not just about you. You have this other person to deal with now too. And this person comes with their own expectations about life and love. So how do you negotiate that?

I'll just say it: Relationships are difficult! We are different animals. And not just male and female. There are fundamental differences in all people because we are all coming from somewhere else. So you have to be willing to work and listen and understand.

And sometimes you have to just accept your differences, and let it go. For example, (and this is a dumb example but you can imagine it on a larger scale) when we first moved in together we had a linen closet. I have always put my pajamas in the linen closet. This is because in the apartments that I have had in my life, I didn't have the dresser space or the closet space. And Lamont was like, "Um, why are you putting your pajamas in the linen closet?" And I said, "Because I put them there, that's where they go."

"Well why do they go there?"

I've come to realize since then that the reason I put them there *is because that way they're in the same place as the dryer sheets and the laundry detergent. And I like my pajamas to smell like laundry detergent. This was something I didn't know about myself. It was a subliminal thing. However, because it bothered Lamont so much, I no longer keep my pajamas in the linen closet. I have since discovered that you can actually take the dryer sheets <u>out</u> of the box and put them in drawers.*

It's kind of a silly example, but the idea is that you have something about yourself that you have always done, and you don't know why you've done it that way, you just have. But now you have this other person who is like a mirror. Who says, "Why have you done this?" And sometimes it's not as simple as dryer sheets. Sometimes it's a heck of a lot more complicated. And he can either say, "Okay, she's going to keep her pajamas in the linen closet and that's the way it's going to be." Or I can say, "Well wait a minute, why do I do that?" Can I let that go? Can I work around it? And can I find a way to make this work better?

Let me tell you something. Being married has totally flipped my perception of myself. Talk about seeing yourself for who you truly are. There are certain traits that I have carried all of my life. For example, it's very hard for me if I'm annoyed or mad at someone, to let it go. I have grievances from the past thirty years. Some of them, when I think about them, put me right back in a negative place and I feel totally justified in feeling the way I do. I am a product of my mother because she is the exact same way. It has been a test for me to be able to try and let things go with Kate. It's really hard, but what I've discovered is that I love Kate so much that I want to be this perfect guy for her. And I try to be. But I also love her so much that I have to show her who I am: Warts and all.

It's hard to truly love somebody just the way they are, but I also think it's something we all deserve.

"Don't go changin'…to try and please me…"

Okay. Stop.

"Mmmmm…mmmm…I take the good times, I take the bad times! I take you just the way you are." That's a good song! Billy Joel. He knows what's up.

I have more fun with Lamont than with anybody in my life. We have so much fun together. We laugh together and I feel like we're just a good team. Even the way we argue is good. We argue all the time. We bicker every day. We rarely have major fights though.

I take a lot of the responsibility for that. I'm very sensitive and I'm also very particular. But so is she. And we're both stubborn.

But we match.

We see through the bullshit.

And we have good sex.

That helps.

VIVE LA FRANCE!

Jacqueline, 87

George, 83

together 2 years

As I ring the buzzer to a retirement community on the outskirts of town, I become very much aware of the strapless sundress I'm wearing. "Uh oh." I think to myself, "This woman is going to think I'm a harlot. She's not going to want to talk to me…why didn't I bring a cardigan or something to cover up?" When the doors slide open, I walk timidly inside, consciously aware of my outfit and my age. I am easily the youngest person in the lobby by about 50 years and the least clothed by far. I am getting looks up, down and sideways. Then I see Jacqueline at the top of the stairs. "Yoo hoo!" She calls, "This way!" I walk up the stairs and she gives me a big hug and a kiss on either cheek as if she has known me my whole life. "What an adorable outfit!" She says. "Come, I want you to meet my boyfriend, George!"

Yes he did!

In any case, we met again and became partners at bridge. Since then we have been playing bridge together, going to movies, going to symphonies, watching DVD's and doing crossword puzzles.

We get together a minimum of three times a week. Sunday, Monday and Tuesday we have established a routine with different things.

But if there's a good film, we'll go another day, and if we feel like a meal we'll go and have a meal together.

And then on the phone. I like the phone and George doesn't, so I mostly call. Isn't that true?

Yes. I have a certain dislike of the telephone.

He gets so many calls from all over.

Well this is the political season, so I get a lot of political calls. Fortunately you can see where they come from these days and so I know those I want to ignore and so on. And there are lots of commercial ones as well. It's funny, I tried to put my phone number on a "do not call" list but it didn't make much difference. I carry my house phone with me in my pocket when I'm at home so I don't have to go and check it constantly. I have it here!

You still have your phone on you? A regular landline phone?

It just happens to be in my pocket. I forgot to leave it. Anyway, I get a lot of phone calls, a lot of regular mail, a lot of emails.

imagining what it would be like having the German army coming down the road, doing what they liked.

The "Goosestep."

Yes, so I wanted to know what it was really like. It was one of those things that I couldn't imagine how bad it must have been. I won't bore you with the details (Jacqueline and I have discussed this at a lot of length) but I think I would much rather go through the bombing again than to be an occupied country.

Anyway, we parted ways. I didn't know anything about George and we said, "Very nice meeting you," and so on. Then two or three weeks later we were invited by that same group to play again. And that second time we parted, I knew a little more about George. I knew he had lost his wife, I didn't know that before, and I had lost my husband too. And George said, when we parted, he said, "Well, if you ever need a partner, call me." Then a few weeks later, my regular partner was taking off for many weeks at bridge. And I said, "I'll call George!" So I did.

That flattered me. We now have a phrase: "Tu etes flatteurs!"

George talks a little French.

Not very much, but that was another attraction actually. I had learnt French through most of my school. Three years in school and five years in high school and then I did scientific French in college. It was a requirement. It used to be the primary diplomatic language and was thought to be a good thing to learn. But I didn't remember enough to impress her anyway.

afternoon and when people can't go they get substitutes. Well we happened to be, individually, substitutes for this group on the same afternoon. I think that happened twice.

The first time I said, "Oh, you're British!" after I talked to him a little. He said, "How did you know?" And I said, "I listen to the BBC!" So we talked for a bit after the game.

I think Jacqueline posed a general question for the group about having accents. And being very fond of language and so on I said, "I'm the only one here without an accent." I guess it was a rather silly answer but I think it peaked her interest. And of course I wanted to speak to her. She has such an attractive accent. It's very…

Different.

Well it makes sure that people know she's different. I was actually listening to her very hard because France and England have not always been very friendly. But I thought to myself, "Here's someone who comes from far away, like me." And I wondered how we'd get on.

When I learned that he had spent the war years in London, I said, "Oh poor you!" Because in France I lived under German Occupation and they told us that they had bombed London. I always felt so sorry for the poor British people…I really did…so I wanted to hear all about it.

Well that was interesting for me too because during World War II, which for us started in 1939, the Germans had pretty much conquered most of continental Europe. They seemed to be so efficient and we thought it was very likely they were going to get us next. I can remember

Mon prenom est…I mean my name is…(I was going to start in French)! Anyway, my name is Jacqueline.

I'm George. And how old am I? Or is she? Or both?

"Me and you and you and me…"

You know, for me, it's a cultural thing, but you never ask a lady her age. Or discuss it.

Oh, I don't mind.

Okay, well I'm eighty-three.

And I'm eighty-seven.

But it makes no difference at this age. I mean if you knew someone at seventy-five and they were with someone who was eighty-five, it wouldn't make any difference. You're just "a bit elderly." And if you can swallow that for yourself you can swallow it for everybody. Isn't that true?

I hope so.

Well at any rate, it's not the sort of thing we talk about very much. Time goes by but you don't have to concentrate on that sort of thing.

Anyway, we met in September of 2010.

Two years ago.

We met by accident.

Yes. We both play bridge and the accident was that there is a bridge group that meets every Wednesday

I don't know why they love him so much.

And it wastes so much of one's time…but that has nothing to do with us. Sorry, we get off track easily…

I lived in Madison, Wisconsin for forty-five years because of my husband's work. I was married for fifty-six years. We went through our "golden anniversary" together. My husband had Parkinson's for fifteen years, but he was in pretty good shape when that happened, so that was nice. It was a good family reunion.

Then in 2004, he became very sick and they wanted to put him in a nursing home. I have two sons in Milwaukee, so we found an apartment where we could be near them and he could be taken care of. But it lasted only three months.

After he passed, I stayed here to be near my sons. I am very comfortable here in this apartment, and George lives in his house down the road a ways.

Yes I have a single family home, which I have been in since 1996. I have two children and they both came here for graduate studies. One went to medical school and one went to business school. My son who went to business school settled here and when I retired I moved here as well.

I was offered to live in George's house if I wanted to. But we are very independent you know.

When we say we see each other about three times a week or sometimes more, it's part of what we decided was a good way to go. For Jacqueline, it wouldn't be sensible for her to come and have a whole house to look after when she's had all the independence that comes with a small apartment that is largely looked after for her.

I'd have to cook and clean. No way!

I think things are better not to be so close. If we were, we would fall over each other and get in each other's way. This way we can be independent and still enjoy each other's existence.

It's nice to see him again at the door, you know?

My previous wife and I were married in 1955. So, let me think, we were forty-five years in that century and then six years in this one, so fifty-one years we were together. But the last year or two my wife was very sick. She had a series of infections that she picked up in the hospital. So we decided to take her home and look after her there. She had six weeks of antibiotics that I had to give her several times a day and I really nursed her as well. We managed to keep her alive for seventeen months, which is longer than they expected. But it was over in October of 2006.

It was very curious. I missed my wife so much. She was such a good person to know and I thought I would never meet someone like that again.

But then that French woman came along!

Well…sometimes you just have to let the charm in. I couldn't ignore it…and I didn't really want to! I think my point is I felt so loyal to my first wife that I was quite settled to the idea that I would never meet anyone else of the same caliber again. It's very surprising really that you can meet someone whom you can love at this point in life.

Jacqueline and I have discussed whether marriage is a good idea or not, but there are a lot of disadvantages at our age. We're not starting a family you see. And it sounds crass, but the legal consequences are not good for one's family. Jacqueline has plans for her family when she passes away and I have some expectations for when I go far, far away again. So it is better not to disturb the relationship with our own families to do something they might not understand and find uncomfortable.

But we get along with the families. George's family is nice to me and my kids are nice to him.

Well, they're nice kids. It is comforting to know that I can be with them and they don't seem to mind having a relative stranger around. That is very reassuring. And my family has absorbed Jacqueline. One of my daughters has a friend who is French, so they get on together.

The one thing Jacqueline and I have in common really is all that wartime stuff. Jacqueline knows the worst of life as well as the best. In my life, I've learnt a lot about how people cope with difficulty. War affects how you think about things, you know? Nobody really understands it now unless they've been there. Talking about the war is really what brought us together. It was at a critical time in my life. For me, World War II was exactly the time I was in high school. I had just missed being in the army, (the class just ahead of me went into to the war) and I have felt guilty ever since. We did do something though: We gave Hitler his second defeat when they started bombing us. He'd had a clear run of success and victory over the rest of Europe before he came to England. But the class I was in felt like, "How did they do this without us?"

You remind me of my husband. He had graduated from college when the war started. He was a chemist and could have very well stayed in Washington DC where he had job in the laboratory. But he wanted to enlist to go fight the Germans. His two brothers were already there and he wanted to be part of that big event. Fortunately he made it. And his brothers too. Can you imagine being a mother having three sons in the war?

He probably could've been excused on the grounds that he already had two brothers fighting.

But then I wouldn't have met him. And I wouldn't be here. Life is strange! I have been very, very lucky in life. I could have been killed many times. And my father, who was a French officer in World War I and World War II, was lucky too. He lived until he was ninety-four.

Our parallel experiences really affect the way we look at things. I'm very intolerant actually of people who don't bear things with a happy heart. There are far worse things than living day to day, and living the life most people live here. It is so different in the rest of the world. Jacqueline and I have a sort of understanding of what the past was like. And although France and England have never really felt themselves close together (historically we've been the great rivals in Europe) there have been so many parallels between us that we have found in common. This is a very strong relationship that we've developed.

We feel very comfortable about being very loving with each other. It's comforting to know that somebody loves you. It's nice.

And I know by now the things that can irritate her.

Like politics!

That is a sore point for her right now.

We are on opposite sides of the spectrum.

Yes, we are polarized, aren't we?

Well, George knows a lot and likes to talk very strongly about it. I am not as involved but I know where I stand.

We have once discussed it and it was enough to upset Jacqueline. So now I know what to avoid. On the whole, I'm concerned with this relationship being positive. If I felt I was being a nuisance I would calmly apologize and offer to let her go. I wouldn't want to be a thorn in her side. We have an understanding that there are certain things that we're not going to touch on and I think it works out very well. It's nice to have a feeling that to some extent you're looking after someone again. I think it's at least as strong as if we'd formally married. I don't think it's necessary for us, at our age, because we're not going to start a new family or anything.

No!

That's just not practical. So the limitations of our social existence are fairly clear. But it would be a big loss if we drifted away from one another. It's curious, if one looks at it with a clear eye, that at our age you could feel this way again.

Yes, it's lovely to be loved again. And I hope it's the same for George.

Well of course it is. Do you think I'd still be coming 'round if it weren't? The feeling that you can care for somebody again is truly remarkable. It matters to me that Jacqueline is happy with our relationship and in the rest of her life that she's content with what she's doing. I try my best to make sure of that.

George is very generous.

I am?

Yes, I mean in his heart. I'm not talking about his pocketbook.

We never talk about money. You sort of let it go with the flow. You work out an accommodation with all the things you need, and if your heart is in the right place you come out with reasonable solutions. I think by our age we've got a pretty good idea of what matters and what doesn't.

We're frugal. Both of us.

We're not frugal, we're <u>careful</u>.

Well I had to be very careful in my youth. I was giving English lessons to be able to buy a stamp to write to the United States. Money was difficult to get for young people in those days, so I learned how to be very careful with money and I have been all my life. I am amazed by the way people rush and go with their cards. To me that is shocking. I never thought of buying anything unless I had the money.

And you see? I am precisely the same way. The way my mother managed her life and her money rubbed off on me. I'm very careful. I like having a nice cushion of resources left. I would feel very uncomfortable buying things without thinking first, "Do I really need this?" And hope that I can do without it. Jacqueline understands that so she doesn't expect me to spend on nonsense.

We are also in a period in our lives where I might need big help tomorrow. And the help is so expensive! It's terrible. I will go through my savings like lightning. So I am very careful. I have to think about my age.

We don't have foolish arguments about trivial things like money. Or, like…well, what sort of things do we not argue about?

Religion.

Oh yes, well we have very different views about religion but we know how to avoid the conflict.

He's a perfect gentleman.

Oh come now. Don't exaggerate, mon ami.

Oui.

I try to speak a little French, just to be polite I suppose.

Yes. Vive la France!

I think in this relationship I have learned to be patient with other people's opinions. I'm pretty opinionated. I've been on the right side of a lot of arguments in my life. And I think I have learned that sometimes it's better to swallow your pride. I'd feel I was failing if I couldn't keep this relationship as productive and as loving as it has been. And it has been loving. I don't understand it at this age, it's not the sort of thing you read about in books, so it has been an interesting experience. I guess Jacqueline must be more patient than most people I've known.

And we share so much.

We share a love of music. We both like classical music.

I like The Beatles!

You do?

I don't understand them, but I like their melodies and their music.

I suppose I might've been more interesting if I'd been a Beatle.

Perhaps.

Ha! But we are very compatible I think. We get on well together. We are well matched and we know what the boundaries are. It's easy to accept those boundaries because having a good relationship with somebody is so valuable.

It's just so lovely to see him. "Ah, here you are again George!"

After all this time.

A MANUAL FOR MARRIAGE

Mary, 51

Andrew, 52

married 28 years

Although she is not related to me, "Aunt Mary" has known me my entire life. Her husband Andrew, a high school teacher/baseball coach, tutored me in Biology when I was fourteen. In exchange, I babysat their two children every Friday night. They are my family. As I begin to set up for the interview Andrew asks, "So what is this about anyway? You just want stories?" "She wants love advice," Mary says confidently. "Hmmm…" Andrew ponders for a moment, "are you sure you want to interview us?"

I'm Andrew. I am fifty-two years old and Mary and I are coming up to our twenty-eighth year of marriage. Our anniversary is October 19th.

I'm Mary and I am fifty-one years old.

We met in college. I was in a fraternity and she was in a sorority. One of her sorority sisters introduced us and it was <u>not</u> love at first sight. It was my fault. I did some dumb things. Let's just say I used to drink…and I don't drink anymore.

Well now we have to finish the story! Andrew made out with my sorority sister on our first date. He took me to a fraternity dance party and then he ended up making out with Sarah Wheezer. And why did I go out with him again? I don't know. I guess he was just that cute. Our actual first date after that…we saw a movie I think.

Yup we saw "Rambo."

There's a romantic movie for ya.

Well, there weren't a lot of movie selections. The movie that was showing at the theatre at that time was "Rambo" and on a first date usually you go see a movie. So that's what we did. Then we went to "The Sweet Onion" for dinner.

That was in '81 or '82. I was a sophomore and Andrew was a junior. And we pretty much dated straight through after that.

We had been dating for two years when I proposed on Christmas day at her house. Her entire family was downstairs and we went upstairs to her room. I had a big box set up there and in the middle of it there was a tiny box with the ring in it. It was my way of catching her off guard. I had already talked to her mom and dad and asked them if I could have her hand in marriage. They were fine with it. It was fun! Then we came back downstairs and made it official to her family.

I wasn't shocked at all. We kind of knew that we were headed down that road, so there was no shock. And then we ended up getting married that next October.

Trying to work around the football schedules.

Yup. Simple livin'! And then we were married for seven years before we had kids.

We tried for a while, but it didn't work very well. The day that we found out we were pregnant, we had an appointment to see a specialist. We had tried for almost two years.

I was thirty when I had Thomas, and thirty-two with Chelsea. Which is still young to me...but most of my friends had their children when they were in their twenties, so I felt old...

I'm glad we waited to have kids because I had to learn how to communicate after we got married. I was the youngest of three brothers so I didn't really learn how to communicate growing up. I think I was probably a burden at times to Mary because I didn't know about communication and compromise.

And we didn't live together before we got married, so that was hard to adjust to.

The door slammed in my face a lot of times those first few years.

Therapy! Therapy's been very good for us. I think we both understand we have to be better communicators in multiple ways. I feel like we're definitely kinder to one another now. You learn over the years that the things you don't like about someone might not change, but they don't bother you in the same way. For example, I kind of hate the way Andrew drives, but it's been twenty-eight years so I have to get over it!

When you first get married you think you know a person...but you don't...not really. So the first three to five years are the years where you're finding out about that individual. It just becomes a little more eye opening...

Relationships are hard. I think people in general can be very selfish. It's very easy to do your own thing. For example, there are some days I get up and I just don't feel like being very nice. I don't always feel like cooking! But sometimes you have to realize that it's not just about you anymore. You have to lose yourself in a way. That sounds kind of bad, but sometimes you have to put away what might be first on your list. I've learned that doing this actually makes me a better person and a stronger person.

Marriage comes with a compromise. Everything that you want to do isn't always going to come first and that's just the way it goes. I think that you grow from that because you understand that you're part of a team. Mary and I constantly help one another out. It's a give and take back and forth. There is no manual for marriage. There is no manual for raising kids. You have to rely on each other and help yourselves get through things.

Pick a good one!

You're going to make mistakes.

And learn how to forgive.

As the wedding vow states, it's an unconditional love. You come into the relationship knowing that your spouse is not going to be perfect. You know that he or she will not always do what they probably should do. But you have to have support and trust and the ability to forgive. Those are some heavy words in that vow. We should probably take a look at them from time to time.

It takes time to get where we are now. In the beginning of our marriage, it definitely wasn't as smooth.

Yup. That door slammed pretty quick sometimes.

It just takes maturity and the knowledge that you are going to stay together. I think sometimes the mind frame in this country is throwaway.

Take the easy way out.

But we know that we're in it for the long run. And people who don't, or cant...no judgment at all...it's just extremely important to us to put one foot in front of the other and stay together.

I also think respect is huge. We both really respect one another for what each of us has done for each other and what each of us has done for the family. Mary, for example, put a lot of her life on hold when we had kids. She decided that she was going to stay home with Thomas and Chelsea instead of putting them in daycare. And I respect her a great deal for deciding to do that.

You can't listen to all those voices in the world that say you have to make the most money and you have to be doing x, y and z for a successful marriage...whatever the formula is that the rest of the world says you need to be a successful couple. You have to know what works for you and really respect one another along the way.

You also have to learn to give one another space. Find things that make you, as an individual, happy. You have to carve out that time or you'll drive each other nuts. Of course, we try to do things together too, but sometimes it doesn't work out too well. We tried taking dance lessons last month…this one always wants to lead and she's not supposed to.

We also have a lot of "couple" friends who we do things with. I think that definitely supports healthy marriages when you're hanging out with other people who have stayed together through good times and bad times.

It's funny, when you're young and you get married, you don't really think of it like, "I'm going to <u>decide</u> to spend the rest of my life with this person." I don't think we had that knowledge or that maturity. We were just too young. I didn't really think to myself, "Okay, self. This is going to be <u>forever</u>." I just married Mary because I thought she was the most honest and caring person that I knew. And her family was the same way. Her dad was one of the most caring individuals I ever had the privilege of knowing, and her mom took me under her wing and accepted me as part of the family from day one. It was easy for me to see that Mary was the person that I respected and loved. The person I fell in love with and am still in love with to this day.

It sounds so cliché, but it really does get better as you get older. Well, it does if you do the work. It doesn't just fall into place, but if you do the work with your spouse, it really does get better.

And of course there are times in life that are harder. Obviously the deaths of our parents were difficult…

It was devastating when my dad got sick…watching him die was awful. And we went through that with both of Andrew's parents. Then we went through a really tough time with our daughter, Chelsea. She had really horrible anxiety when she first started college…

It's hard because you don't know what you're doing sometimes. There's no manual and you just hope you're doing the right thing.

I'm really glad I wasn't a single parent and that Andrew was so supportive. He is constantly thanking me for being a good mom and he really appreciates me and recognizes me. Every night we pray together out loud and we thank each other for things that happened during the day and we pray for the kids. It's really fun. It's kind of like a funny, rambling conversation with God. It's probably not your traditional prayer that most people have, but it's nice. At the end of the night we always recognize each other, thank one another, and thank God that we have each other.

It's not easy. It's hard work. It's not something you can say, "Oh, I'll put this on a shelf somewhere for a few weeks and get back to it whenever." It's a daily ritual and you have to be a part of it.

And if you are, it's really rewarding.

Exactly…but if she talks about my driving anymore, she's out the door!

QUIET TIME

Catherine, 30

Steve, 30

married 4 years

I attended college with Catherine and Steve. At twenty-five, they were the first among my friends to get married.

You go first.

Okay. My name is Catherine and I'm…(deep breath)…Thirty. Years. Old.

Aw, we have to say our ages?

Yeah, we have to give our ages away. Thirty, we're thirty.

I'm Steve and I'm thirty as well.

We've been married for four years, but we've been dating for nine.

That makes it real.

We met in school. In the theatre department. I had a <u>huge</u> crush on him. Like, huge, huge, <u>huge</u> crush. It's really cheesy, but from the first second I saw him I was like, "Who is <u>that</u>?" I don't know. I just really liked him before we even spoke to one another. And it was a really long time before we even spoke! But from the moment I saw him, every time after that, I was just like, "Oh my gosh there's that guy again…Oh! There he is again." We started to pass each other in the hallways. We got into a routine where we would just say "hi" whenever we'd pass. Finally, sophomore year, we were going to have a class together. On the first day, our professor looked at Steve and asked him why he was there.

This is really embarrassing because I liked Catherine a lot and was so excited to have a class with her. So when he asked me why I was there, I came up with this really profound answer. "Oh, I really want to be an actor because…" And I had these big philosophical reasons why I felt like this was my passion and my destiny…blah, blah, blah. And he was like, "No. Why are you <u>here</u> in this class? You're not supposed to be here. You need to take these pre-requisite classes before you can be approved to be here." So, I um…got up and left the classroom. It was awkward.

We were so close to getting to know one another better and then he got sucked out of class! I was so mad. Anyway, we met our freshman year but we didn't start dating till our junior year 'cause Steve had a girlfriend.

Yup. Catherine's a little home wrecker.

I didn't steal you!

No, I know. It was totally my choice. And Catherine and I hardly talked to each other before this happened. It wasn't super flirtatious or anything. I think we were actually trying to avoid each other.

Well, I didn't really know his situation. I knew he had a girlfriend, but I didn't know they had been together for five years. When I heard that, I was devastated. Like, "What am I doing? I need to stop liking this guy."

So I broke up with this other girl and that was tough because I not only felt like I was breaking up with her, I felt like I was breaking up with her family as well. I actually spent more time at her house than I did my own back in high school. And not just in the basement or whatever kids do…I was having dinners with her family and going on vacations with them…it was pretty serious. Catherine and I both come from parents who went through messy divorces, so it was just nice being around a solid family you know?

Anyway, I knew that I liked this other girl, and I loved her family, but I knew that I didn't love <u>her</u>.

Especially after I met Catherine. Catherine and I are very like-minded. Some couples talk about how they are complete opposites and then some couples are the same. I think this other girl and I were opposites. Catherine and I are more similar. And I don't know why, but for some reason I thought that would work better for me. It's been working out so far!

Right after Steve broke up with this girl, he and I got cast in a show together. One afternoon before rehearsal we wanted to go through our lines. But when we showed up at the theatre, we decided to get some food instead. It wasn't an official date. It was like a trick date. And of course we didn't do any work.

Then we made out!

No, there was more to it than that! After rehearsal, everyone left and we talked for a while…and then we made out.

So after we made out, it was like, well, we're in deep now. I kissed her so she should probably be my girlfriend and stuff.

After we graduated, I went to Purdue for grad school and Steve stayed home and was working full time. One day Steve said, "Let's go back to school and walk around and talk about memories." And I'm an idiot and we're cheesy, so I was like, "Okay!" But I totally didn't see the proposal coming. We were just walking around the theatre and all of a sudden, Steve got down on one knee and proposed. It was so perfect. But the rest of that day was actually not very fun.

I had talked to Catherine's mom beforehand and asked her if it was cool if I proposed. Basically I was trying to do the traditional thing. Her mom said, "Absolutely not." Obviously I asked Catherine anyway.

We were going to get engaged regardless. We just wanted her mom's blessing.

She didn't want me to get married.

She thought we were too young and I think she still wanted a Greek guy for Catherine. Catherine's sister had a fiancé who converted to Greek Orthodox, and I didn't want to do that, so that was hard. We've gone to church but we're not super religious. We're not "church goers" I guess.

As we were driving home my mom called. In a low voice she said, "Did he do it?" When I told her he had, she left the house, stayed with my grandparents and wouldn't talk to me. She made me take my wedding ring off in church every Sunday. She didn't want me to tell the family.

I had a huge problem with that, for obvious reasons. So our engagement wasn't exactly what you would call a fairy tale. It was extremely rough those first few months. But we didn't care. We did what we wanted.

I remember lying in bed for two days straight after Steve proposed. I was so numb and depressed. It was a really rough time. Not what you're supposed to be feeling when you just get engaged.

But we were engaged for three years. It's not like we were going to get married that next week!

And she knew that! Steve was going to school in England and I was going to school in Indiana. When we were both done with our programs, then we were going to get married. But we wanted that commitment to each other while we were so far away.

Being engaged is different than, "I've got this

girlfriend back home." I wanted a stronger commitment and Catherine did too.

That was such a dark time.

It was harder for Catherine than it was for me I think.

Well I was in this program where I didn't have a lot of close friends. Steve was in England meeting awesome people, and I was stuck in the cornfields with the three people I knew. Those were very difficult years. The family didn't really accept us and we were dealing with the distance as well.

One good thing that came from being so far apart was that we learned how to use Skype. I don't know when Skype came out, but it was new to me. We went about a week without talking and then once we got Skype up and running, we could talk to each other and see each other every day.

It made a huge difference.

My grandfather was in the war and was stationed in England for almost two years. He was only allowed a letter a week to my grandma. They were married for fifty years. I would always think about that while we were apart. I knew if I could see and talk to Catherine every day, we'd be okay.

One thing from the distance that I found to be kind of nice was that I really got to see Steve grow. When you're with someone every day you can't really see them change that much. You're not really aware of people changing when you're around them all the time. But being apart for so long, I could really see Steve develop. I got to actually see Steve grow and witness him mature.

Ahem. I have always been very mature.

If we were together every day, I might not have gotten to see that and notice or appreciate it…but it was still crappy being apart for those years.

Yup. So our engagement was pretty terrible, and then the wedding was a huge stress. The tradition of a wedding itself is an enormous nightmare. You're basically putting on this huge production and paying a lot of money for absolutely no reason! Yay!

We were hungry that day too. That was part of the problem. We both have to eat regularly.

And we had to smile for all these stupid pictures. Smiling that much hurts your face! It was so annoying.

It was a nice day though.

In terms of the memories and the pictures, yes, it was great. Twenty years from now, we will be able to look at the pictures and it'll look amazing. But I'll tell you what; the next morning we were train wrecks.

I have never felt that bad. To this day I have <u>never</u> felt that bad. Our bodies just ached. I guess from all the hugging and the dancing…

And the drinking and the lack of food. The standing and the smiling…it was awful. Oh, and then there was our honeymoon! That <u>sucked</u>.

It didn't suck!

Yeah it did. It was my fault.

It wasn't.

No, I'm gonna take the hit on this one. We went to Mackinac Island.

Yeah, and paid extra for the "lake view" room.

There's this old mansion that is on the back of the island, far away from the touristy stuff. They have these horse drawn carriages to take you there. So I thought to myself, "That could be romantic right? It's on a cliff and there will be sunsets! We'll get the best suite with the best view. We'll just hang out and have a good time!" Let me tell you, it was not as advertised!

We got there and almost left the first night.

Well, you would think the horses would be cool right? No. You get in the carriage and the horse tries to take you there, but it's on the other side of the island. We were going so slow that at one point this old lady on a motorbike zoomed right by us. This horse was tired. He had to rest all the time. When we got to the top of the hill he had to rest for like five minutes. And he was pooping everywhere.

It was pretty funny.

So we got there and literally the "lake view" is a tiny window that's barely big enough to look through. You can't open it. And it's in the corner so you can't see it unless you physically walk to the corner and look out.

It was an attic window so it was cut into the wall.

It was really lame.

We just ate a lot of fudge and a lot of ice cream. And came back disappointed.

So all those things that were supposed to be great, were pretty awful: The engagement, the wedding, the honeymoon...but it's more the day-to-day stuff that people stress out about, or personality differences that people worry about, that we don't have problems with. It's great. Every night is like a sleepover. We're always having fun. And then in the morning if I want to get up and eat ice cream for breakfast, it's cool! She's not my mom! It's pretty awesome to not have your mom around. It doesn't feel like it's been nine years at all.

I'm kind of in a transitional phase in my life right now. I'm working a lot of odd jobs and going kind of crazy, and I feel like I love Steve even more when my life feels like it's in shambles. He's rooted and stable. Having that sort of stability you can count on when everything else is chaotic means a lot.

When we're busy and focused on other things, we don't pay as much attention to each other. We try to make time, but sometimes we'll go months and not even really connect to one another.

When that happens, we usually acknowledge it and realize that we need a day for us. Whenever we start to bicker or if there's tension, we realize that we aren't connecting and we make the effort to try and spend more time together.

I think we make a big effort to try to do that. Maybe we put a lot of pressure on ourselves because we both come from divorced families. We want to work hard on our relationship so we don't end up like our parents. So we talk about things before they become a big deal.

Catherine has a habit of shutting off when she's really mad. Like, "I'm just going to go for a walk or hang up on you."

It's the Greek blood! We slam doors and hang up on people. We're crazy.

But I've made it clear that behavior doesn't fly with me. You can go into another room and I'll just follow you. I'm not going anywhere till we figure this out. I like to sort things out right away. I think if you don't, problems can grow into something they aren't originally. Tension can build up over years if you hold onto grudges. I think we've always flushed things out right away. We don't just say, "Oh, we'll deal with this later."

It's also amazing what the words "I love you" can do. Today, for instance, we had a little argument.

We hadn't eaten.

Yes, that's how it usually starts. So we were bickering a little bit and I was feeling down and suddenly Steve said, "I love you," and it all went away. Whatever we were arguing about didn't matter anymore. It was behind us. I think one of the strengths in our relationship is that we can talk through anything. I wouldn't necessarily say we're "talkers" though. We also really like quiet time.

Oh yeah. I need to be quiet. I think most people are uncomfortable with silence. It's unusual to find somebody that understands the need for "quiet time."

And that doesn't necessarily mean "alone time." Sometimes I just need to be quiet. We can still be around one another, just...don't talk to me.

It's really nice to eat your meal and not have to talk.

I never realized that I prefer that. Sometimes I feel like I get overloaded with life. It's really nice to be with someone who understands that.

I love quiet time. It's the best!

Yeah, we need quiet time. And naps.

We're officially old.

DO YOU LOVE ME?

Eleanor, 81

Gordon, 78

married 56 years

This old house. The stories it could tell. The sounds of my childhood awaken within me. I have so many memories here. Christmases and Thanksgivings that are full of turkey, stuffing, rolls and cranberry sauce. Aunts and uncles and generations of cousins packed into the basement opening presents. These are memories that I treasure. And this is home to me.

My name is Eleanor and I'm eighty-one years old. Gordon and I have been married for fifty-six years. We've known each other for sixty.

I'm her husband, Gordon.

We met at Calvin College. We were in a choir together. I was a senior and Gordon was a freshman. I lived out on a lake with a family working for my room and board, so I took the bus to and from school.

It's a miracle that we even got to know each other really because I lived on campus and she was off campus working for this family. But we had rehearsals every week for this choir and Sunday mornings we would sing live on the radio. Every Sunday morning at 8:30 we'd sing an introduction to this service, then a guy from Chicago spoke, and then we sang at the end. We'd all go out for a walk afterwards. Well, I saw this shapely sort of woman who dressed nicely and had these beautiful blue eyes. We soon became friends but I don't remember ever having "dates." We just hung out.

One time we were on a bus choir tour. Gordon was lying in the aisle on some suitcases next to me and reached up to hold my hand. I think that solidified our relationship.

We sang at a lot of churches. And we did go to one concert together. Johnnie Ray. He was an early pop singer that used to lay on the floor and gyrate all over the place. I didn't have a car, so we must've taken the bus or something. But the funny thing is, that kind of music isn't even the kind of music we liked!

Then after I graduated, I went home to Iowa. I didn't want to put pressure on our relationship. I felt that Gordon had his whole college career ahead of him and I was leaving to teach in Massachusetts anyway. I thought it was only fair to him that he had his own life in college without me.

And fair to her so she could date some other guy!

But we didn't take a break. Not really. We wrote each other every night. Which is really something because now we have these boxes and boxes of letters. We didn't see one another for a full year. It wasn't until after that year that Gordon came to see me in the summertime and I stopped in Chicago to see him at Christmas. I dated one other person at this time. It wasn't very memorable…and now he's dead, so I guess it's a good thing I picked Gordon!

In 1954 Eleanor moved back to Grand Rapids to teach. I still had a couple of years to finish school. Then on April 1, 1956 we got engaged. On April fools day! Eleanor's parents were there the weekend before and I had asked her dad's permission. I think he was nervous because ministers don't make that much money.

He was afraid his daughter wasn't going to be taken care of.

So we got on the bus and we went to a place called "Safees Restaurant" for dinner. I don't think she knew I was going to ask her. But I asked her if she'd marry me and gave her a ring. I worked a whole summer just to pay for that ring. Then the waitress said, "You dummy, why didn't you put it in a glass of champagne and serve it to her?" I didn't know any better. I was about 22 I guess, and she was 25. So we got engaged in April and we were married in August.

The wedding was in Pella, Iowa, so it was quite a ways for people from Chicago to come. We had four attendants each. It was a really nice, big wedding. We had ham buns and cake afterwards.

We took a week for our honeymoon and went to South Dakota. Went to Mt. Rushmore and all that. It's where my folks had gone on their honeymoon.

I thought a lot about marriage before we got married. I believed that it was a commitment in spite of the good times and the bad. But if you think about it, when you get married to someone you don't really know the person until you're actually living with them. You don't know all those little quirky things. We are very different people but we like a lot of the same things. We like music, we like art, we like going to museums, concerts and movies.

But we really like to travel. I think we're the best together when we travel. We've been all over the world. That's expanded us and also given us knowledge about other people and cultures. We've gone to Europe, Africa, Japan…all over the world and she trusts that it'll be okay.

And if it isn't quite okay, it'll be over in a year or so.

Eleanor is not a very risky person and yet, she was willing to risk a lot by doing all these things with me. We took a trip in 1988 for seven months to travel around the United States on a sabbatical. We lived in monasteries, convents, Buddhist temples, Hindu ashrams…her friends thought she was kind of crazy. Not every woman would be willing to do that. We lived in a car and in little tiny rooms. Some of those rooms weren't big enough to change your mind in. We thought we'd either be divorced or better friends after seven months of doing this together. And we were better friends I think.

I'm grateful for all the traveling we've done. Growing up we didn't have culture around. It's not that my parents weren't interested…it just wasn't a high priority. But when I went to college I took a course in art. I've always enjoyed traveling, learning about art and going to museums.

But we always had a home to come home to. We've lived in this house for forty-nine years. We like creating a home. This is <u>us</u>. Not everybody likes what we have, but this is our stuff. There was nothing here when we moved in, and now we have flowers and trees in our yard. This is who we are. We like putting art on the walls. Some of it is kind of weird. Sometimes we feel like we're still college kids.

I love our home. We've done so much and seen so much but I love being home. Seeing the kids grow up has meant so much more to me than anything we have ever experienced or seen traveling. I've never regretted being a stay-at-home mom. And then I also got to watch the grandchildren grow up too. Those were very rich experiences for me.

It's different for kids today getting married. You think about what your roles will be and all that. I think in our day, we just knew what the roles were. The guy worked and the woman stayed home. Not everybody had that, but in a way we didn't think about it. It was only later in life that I started thinking, "Hey, maybe I should be doing some of the things that she's been doing the last fifty years."

Gordon was gone a lot and I think he regrets that. I do think it might've been better if he had been home some nights and I went out but that's just the way it was…

I was busy getting the career and was preoccupied a

lot. I think one of the things that is a danger in marriage is you take one another for granted. And I think maybe I did that because Eleanor is so good at all kinds of stuff. She's so darn efficient. She takes care of everything right away and she's such a great cook. Just imagine how many meals she's cooked in fifty-six years!

Not anymore. I'm tired.

I was in seminary from 1956 to 1960 and we had two sons during that time. Then we went to Amsterdam for my graduate studies and our daughter was born there. So here I am, twenty-nine years old, and Eleanor is thirty-something, and I don't have a job yet. People in Chicago used to say to my mom, "What's Gordon doing now?" And she'd say, "Well he's going to seminary" or "Well, he's in Europe studying…"

"Ohhh…that's interesting…"

You see, most my friends had gotten out of high school and college and had been working ever since. They owned businesses now. They had big homes and families and everything. And here I was still in school. People didn't think what I was doing was "interesting" at all. They thought it was dumb. So at last, when I was twenty-nine, we moved here and I got a job at the chapel.

And we had our youngest daughter when I was thirty-four.

Eleanor is a very supportive person. I had this crazy job, and what she provided was a haven at home of peace and quiet and gentleness. Well, it wasn't always quiet with four kids. It was nuts. I don't know how Eleanor learned this, but she was such a good mother.

Sometimes I think I was too patient.

No. You were such a good mother and an even better grandmother. I learned how to be a parent from you.

Oh, you can be really patient and accepting with grandkids. I think you should be grandparents first and then parents. That way you can be involved, but then you get to go home!

Eleanor is very patient. I can be impatient and judgmental and so on. But she's so patient and positive. She's principled but compassionate. She has her own ideas about what her beliefs are and yet cares about people who differ from her. I think that's a really wonderful quality to have, and she's shown that time and time again.

She's also frugal. If not for her we'd probably be bankrupt fifteen times over. She takes care of all the money in the house. She writes the checks. I'm too much of a procrastinator and too A.D.D. probably. I'm all over the place. But she's so efficient. If a bill comes, it's paid.

It's true. I can't stand when papers pile up. I'm very efficient and Gordon's not, but we sort of fit together in a way because we're so different.

She's kind of quiet and I'm kind of noisy. I'm controlling, she's more free.

I hold my own.

Another thing we share is our spiritual life. I think that has been really important in our marriage.

We do morning and evening prayers every day together.

We share our faith. We worship together. We sometimes sit together after our morning prayers and talk. Sometimes about theology. Or about the bible. We talk about death and how to prepare for that. Our faith has meant oodles to us. That's the rock bottom of our relationship I think.

Our faith also gives us a sense of belonging to one another and to our spiritual community.

And that doesn't mean we're together all the time. We definitely have our own separate lives.

But it takes awhile for a relationship to get to where we are.

People think you get what we have instantly. I've had people come to me who want to get married after being together for a few months. They say, "We just get each other completely." And I say, "You sure must be superficial people." Nobody can know another person completely. I've been married for over fifty years and I still don't know Eleanor completely. It takes a while and it takes work. Marriage isn't easy. It takes work to make a relationship go.

I think people aren't always willing to work in a marriage. They give up kind of easily.

I remember a couple came to me, they had been married for seventeen years, and they weren't doing well. They said that they just "didn't know one another anymore." Then they decided to make a re-commitment to the people that they <u>were</u>, rather than the people they used to be when they got married. Because you grow and develop separately…it's inevitable. Maybe every five or ten years, people need to check in with one another. Assess where they're going and if they're going along together because you make some vows, you know? Sometimes it might be good to look them over once and a while.

I think just a pat, a hug, a kiss, saying, "I love you" once in awhile…that helps.

I always think of "Fiddler on The Roof" when Tevye asks Golde if she loves him.

Oh, that's such a great song: "Do You Love Me?"

And she says, "What do you mean? I wash your clothes and do all this stuff for you…" I think you can show love with all the things you <u>do</u> for a person, but I also think saying it is very important.

So here we are together after fifty-six years, full of gratitude I think. We feel so blessed.

We really do. I look at our whole family and not just my children, but my grandchildren and my in-laws. I just love them all. We are very, very grateful.

BOY SCOUT

Jennifer, 36

Marc, 37

married 12 years

Jennifer and Marc bring their two little boys over to my place one Friday evening after work. My mother distracts the kids with puzzles and banana bread while I steal Jennifer and Marc for a quick chat in our backyard. "Can we have gin and tonics?" Jennifer asks me. "Your mom promised we could have gin and tonics…and I think we'll be more interesting with gin and tonics."

Hey, did you find Jason's birthday present?

Nope.

Did you <u>look</u>?

I mean there's nothing in my room. Nothing in my closet. I didn't see anything in the basement, but things have been moved around down there. I looked in the secret room and back in your closet.

Okay. Well, we'll worry about that later…

We lost our son's birthday present.

He's two, he won't know.

It's not like we promised him…it's not like he made a list for Christmas or anything. He's too young to do that.

Yeah, he won't know…

Anyway, I'm Marc and I'm thirty-seven.

I'm Jennifer and I'm thirty-six.

We got married in July of 2000.

So we've been married for twelve years. But we met our junior year of college. I was nineteen and Marc was twenty.

We lived in student co-ops and our houses were next door to one another.

The window of my room faced the window of his room…so I could easily stalk him.

She makes it sound like we were spying on each other.

Well it helped that I could see into his room because I always knew when he was home. So I knew I could come over and bother him!

I lived in the co-op for a year before Jennifer moved in next door. Her co-op didn't have an industrial kitchen so they ate with us. We saw each other a lot during dinner.

I had been keeping my eye on Marc for a while. It was really weird to come from a small high school where I knew everyone and knew everything about everyone, to a college that was huge and everyone was a complete stranger. There's a lot of uncertainty when you go from a really small environment to a really big environment in terms of the people you meet. So the people in the co-op become your friends because you have a lot of contact with them. You see how they treat one another and how they work in the co-op, like if they do the job they're assigned to or not. Marc was the "fix it" guy. I remember one time in the middle of the night he had to go to Meijer to get some plumbing supplies. I remember thinking that he seemed really resourceful, kind of like my dad.

Marc and I played on the same intramural soccer team. We played mostly fraternities, which didn't have a lot of girls and not a lot of skilled players. There was a <u>lot</u> of roughhousing. During a game, Marc and I were both going for the ball, and he accidentally elbowed me across the face. It hurt and I had two black eyes, but I thought I was fine. Then after a few hours it became clear that he had broken my nose, so in the middle of the night he took me to the hospital.

I took Jennifer to the ER and we stayed there for

<u>forever</u> because a broken nose doesn't qualify as an emergency apparently.

They make you wait for like five hours and then basically tell you they cant do anything. I guess they kind of realigned it. Squished it back into place.

Then we went out for breakfast…and she was a raccoon for two weeks.

Yeah I was really ugly. I guess after that I kind of had an inkling that Marc liked me. But of course I was all seventh grade about it. So I would talk to other people I knew in his co-op and ask them what he thought of me. It was stupid because I knew he was dating someone else…but then I basically cornered him and told him that we should go on a walk. I confronted him and said, "I hear you might like me, is it true?"

This is after we walked around for like an hour…

Neither of us wanted to broach the issue because we both were dating other people. Then we pretty much confessed to one another that we were interested but we had these other people we had to deal with first. And then we kissed.

There was a girl who I had dated the year before and she was living in Iowa.

And I was with someone who I had dated over the summer but then he went back to school in Texas. So both of us were in long distance relationships that were going to end anyway. After we dealt with our "significant others," we had our first date.

We walked around downtown and bought friendship bracelets.

Yeah that was really dorky. They were bright neon. Oh so pseudo 80's...even though it was the 90's...

I think the first "real" thing we did was pick pumpkins with Jennifer's sister.

Right. Trial by fire! Forget having nice romantic dates together, I just introduced him to my family! We went to my parent's house to pick up my little sister and then straight to the pumpkin patch to pick pumpkins.

But then we had a proper date at that Indian restaurant, "Raja Rani."

Which was great because then I discovered that he liked Indian food.

Then the next night I tried to cook her dinner.

Oh, he did! With the "Bubba Gump Shrimp Company" book! So here I knew he could repair sewage pipes, he liked to do outdoorsy things like pick pumpkins, he liked Indian food and he could cook. This was looking fairly promising.

It's not who I am, but it's what I was projecting. It's who I wanted to be. I did a pretty good job of fooling her.

That first year we also went on a camping trip together. I needed to get away from school for a little bit and Jennifer asked if she could come. I said, "Sure." This was in the late fall, like a month or two after we had started dating. I used to be a boy scout so I was thinking I would sleep in a tent and bring all of my supplies in a backpack...

And I was thinking that it was going to be a little more comfortable than that. More like car camping…or in a cute, little cottage.

So then I asked her what she wanted to bring for food.

And I was like, "Well, when we go camping with my dad he makes us pepper steak and fajitas."

I was so confused. I didn't understand how he carried all of this raw meat and kept it cold.

And I was like, "In a cooler of course!"

We definitely had different camping styles. But since then we've grown a little bit. That time we ended up renting a cottage, but Jennifer will now do back-country camping with me.

Yes, with bears.

And I've done more car and state park camping.

We've definitely started to do more things that the other person enjoys. We've broadened our horizons. I think Marc may recognize that our vacations may not be exactly what he's planned, but I in turn am willing to give some new things a chance.

After we graduated, we moved to Boston together. Marc's sister lived in Boston and I got a job there. It was during that year that I started giving ultimatums like, "I want to be engaged by the year 2000."

But I already had a ring and she didn't know that…

He told me he had a ring in a security deposit box but I didn't believe him. It turns out it was true!

On the 18th of December we went out to an Italian restaurant on the north side of Boston. I had made a fortune cookie that said, "Will You Marry Me?"

I think the fortune said, "Jennifer, will you marry me?" With appropriate commas.

I kept saying, "Do you want dessert?" Because it was Chinese New Year…

And I love fortune cookies. So anyway, I opened it and read it and it was so shocking. At first I was like, "Whoa! This has my name on it, can you believe it?!?" And then I was like, "Wait a minute, what does it say?" And then I was like, "Wait a minute, who put this in here??" It took me awhile to process the whole thing. I mean, how did you even get that in there?

I bought a whole bag of fortune cookies from the grocery store and used tweezers to pull the fortune out. Then I folded mine and put it in there. I had to find the perfect one that was easy to maneuver. But it took a while.

I just laughed a whole lot and then I said, "Well can I answer you now?" And then I said yes. It was another year and a half before we got married. I was still really young. I was twenty-four when we got married and Marc was twenty-five.

We were the first of all of my friends to get married. And after we got married, we waited a fairly long time to have kids. We knew we wanted kids, but because we were so young, there were other things we wanted to do first.

So when we were ready to have kids it was really frustrating, because we couldn't. The whole miscarriage thing was really stressful. It was hard individually. It was hard for us together...

I think the hardest thing was that we had been married for such a long time. A lot longer than any of our friends. We wanted to have kids and had been trying to have kids for a while. Some of our friends who didn't seem like they wanted to have kids all that much were suddenly having kids.

They got pregnant really easily and never seemed to have any problems.

That was difficult.

It was hard because I <u>really</u> wanted it and I knew Marc wanted to be a dad. But there wasn't a lot we could do about it. I think in some ways going through that made us closer. I don't think it drove us apart at all.

I had two miscarriages. They pretty much told me it was never going to happen unless I had fertility treatments. And I just wasn't sure I wanted to go that route. When I finally did get pregnant and it did stick, we had actually decided on adoption. We had turned in all the paperwork and the day we turned in the non-refundable two thousand dollar check, was the day we found out I was pregnant with Marcus. But even then, I was afraid I was going to have another miscarriage since that was what had happened every other time. So when it didn't happen, I think we were all the more thankful. It sounds dorky, but it really felt like we had been blessed. Marc's dad had passed away while all this was happening so I really felt that Marcus's spirit and Marc's dad sort of crossed paths. I think his dad infused some of his spirit in Marcus and was sort of reincarnated.

When Marcus was born it really seemed that way.

He's a lot like my dad.

During the pregnancy I didn't complain at all. I didn't care how sick I was or how upset I felt or how weirdly hormonal, this is what we had wanted and what we had waited such a long time for. I just hoped at the end of it all we would have a healthy baby.

And then our son Jason was even more of a crazy miracle.

We had been told we would <u>never</u> be pregnant again without medical intervention. And then Jason just popped up!

I still think I was out of town when that all happened.

You were not out of town! But again, contrary to what modern science told us, these babies happened. They were little miracles. They probably didn't happen at exactly the right times (we were not prepared for Jason at all) but I don't know that we ever would have been.

She did a great job being pregnant.

Didn't I? A lot of people complain a lot. They have every right to, but I <u>was</u> pretty awesome.

She's good at growing babies.

I think when you're first in a relationship it's all about yourself and having fun. Doing fun activities and sharing stuff. But then after you get married it's also about finances and insurance and taxes and having kids. If those are the things that you want, I think your relationship becomes deeper in a lot of ways. But those things come with challenges. Doing your taxes is not fun and worrying about your finances and arranging your bank accounts?

Not fun. But I think that it makes your relationship meaningful in a different way. In a deeper way. Some days it's hard to remember to insert fun into your life, but I think if you have a good foundation of those things to start with, you can bring them forward into the rest of your relationship.

I think the most challenges come with having children. When it's just the two of you, you have all that other stuff sure, but it's still all about you…

And the dogs…I made him have dogs.

I had a dog before we met!

You had, like, half a dog.

You know, a friend of ours was thinking about getting married a few years ago and I remember he asked us why we decided to get married. I still remember Jennifer's answer. She said that she was a better person with me than without me, and I think the same is definitely true in my case.

Marc is such a good guy. I am a better person with him. I have achieved more and I have challenged myself more. I have had deeper and more meaningful experiences because Marc is with me. So ultimately, it sounds like a selfish reason. You know, "I'm a better person" and "I've had a happier life because of him." But hopefully I've done the same in his case.

She has.

Anyway, I could tell that Marc was a good person. That in his heart he was an honest person. That he was loyal.

And I thought she was funny, smart and beautiful.

I mean Marc was really cute too. But it was more than that. I could tell that he had a good sense of humor and was quirky. He was a good friend and he did the work he was supposed to do in the co-op. I could tell we had a lot in common and that he would be a good fit for me and my family and what I wanted my life to be.

Wow. Before you even knew me you had this all figured out?

Well, this is why I observed you from afar in the co-op for two months. I couldn't just date all willy-nilly.

In case you haven't figured this out, Jennifer is more of the planner in our relationship. I just thought she was hot. But I was a lot more self-focused before I met Jennifer. I was more of a procrastinator and didn't really think things through as much. I am nowhere near as qualified and as capable as Jennifer but I've gotten somewhat better at that.

Marc is my moral compass. Not that I am an immoral person, but he definitely is true north when it comes to social and personal issues. He never has a negative thing to say about anybody. I am much more likely to be emotional and judgmental. I think we're a good compliment for each other.

I don't think I'm a moral compass.

No, it's true. I call you "Boy Scout" for a reason.

PROM NIGHT

Patricia, 83

married 46 years to Emmitt, deceased.

"So you're coming to Detroit with me tomorrow morning?" Dad asks. "Sure!" I say. "Okay, I'll drop you off at Grandma's around eight and then I'll pick you up when I'm done at work." "Great…and what time will that be exactly?" I realize then and there that I have never spent more than a few hours alone with Grandma before. Certainly never a whole day. I was nervous! After I was done with the interview, what would we talk about? What would we do? It was a day I will remember for the rest of my life.

I am eighty-three years old and I think I was about twenty-one when I met Emmitt. His brother introduced me to him. I worked with his brother 'cause I was a teacher at that time. I had heard about the Bowen boy who was finally home from the service. I was curious, because he had been in the service and was missing in action.

When I was in high school I had a boyfriend who was in the service…not a real boyfriend I guess, but a friend who was close. He was missing too. His name was Fred. He didn't come back. He was gone. They were looking for him and looking for him, and he never made it back.

I had heard about Emmitt through his mother when the war was going on. She would always say, "He's not hurt. My boy's coming home." And he did come home eventually. But he did get hurt. He wasn't a complainer, but he did get hurt. We were married for forty-six years and it was a long time before I realized what he had been through. It was a long time before I realized how hurt he had been…

We never talked about it, but he was a Prisoner of War for three years. He would always write about his experiences. He had just about finished his book before he passed. But he never completed it.

So I knew about the Bowen boy, but I never asked questions about him. I had a full life and I was busy. I used to see him sometimes passing my home with his brother, but I guess I wasn't too curious. And I wasn't the type of girl who was going to be too flirty-flirty. I just enjoyed myself. I did a lot of reading and listening to music. I taught. I went to school. Things like that.

But his brother introduced me to him and we went out on several dates together. Our first date was at "Little Harlem" in

Montgomery, Alabama. I guess you could call it a nightclub. We talked about our school and our teachers. We both went to the same college. He went during the year and I went during the summer when I wasn't teaching. So we discussed our teachers and the classes we were taking. And we danced. Did the jitterbug and that kind of stuff. The kids always looked at me funny when I told them daddy used to dance. "Yeah, but mom, daddy had trouble walking." I'd say, "Well he didn't <u>always</u> have trouble walking!" He was a handsome man! He used to dance and did all that kind of stuff.

We had a lot of fun. Emmitt owned his own car so we often took long rides. We took in a lot of movies. Went to see a lot of bands together. We enjoyed music and things like that.

I was so carefree. I didn't ever feel that you "owned" somebody else just by dating them. I just enjoyed life. I think that young girls these days get so attached. Want to get married and do this and that. Why? Just enjoy yourself! I loved people and I enjoyed being around people. I didn't think about getting married to somebody so he would take care of me. I never felt that way.

But Emmitt was so serious! I wasn't ready for all that. He wanted me to get a ring right away. I'd say about two or three months after we started dating. I wasn't quite ready for that commitment, so I didn't accept the ring at first. Then we got more serious and we both was going to the same college so we decided maybe getting married would be the right thing to do. We hadn't been going together more than six or eight months.

I think we fulfilled each other's needs. We needed each other and it was time for us to get married, so we did. I wondered how I would really enjoy being married, 'cause I had enjoyed the good old single life. I mean, really, it was a lot of fun!

We cared about each other. We were young, but we loved each

other and enjoyed each other. Of course we had our ups and downs and misunderstandings. I can't ever remember us breaking up though. Like people do these days; break up and get back together. Before we got married I can't remember no arguments. I really can't when I look back over it. Because he was a kind person. A sweet person. And he was reliable. If he said he'd be somewhere at a certain place at a certain time, he would always be there.

We had a quiet wedding. We were in college then and we went to school the next day. It was fun though. We got married at a preacher's home, not at the courthouse. But it could've been that. It really didn't matter. There was four of us there. Me and him, his brother and my best girlfriend. No family. My family was fine with that because they knew I was going to school and I had one year to finish. We thought maybe later we might do something. Maybe we'd have a big wedding. But we never did. We really didn't care about it too much.

His mother died before the wedding so Emmitt took my mother for his. He always called her mom. And she loved him a lot.

It's kind of unusual isn't it? How he and I got together. But, really, it was nice. We liked each other and respected each other and so on. I wasn't quite as popular on the campus as he was because he was a fraternity guy. I didn't have time to join a fraternity because I worked during the year and went to school in the summer. But that year after we were married, my senior year, I decided to go back to college full time.

I hadn't planned on children much. Emmitt had planned on being a doctor and we were going to move to California. We weren't going to have kids for a long, long time. I don't remember what changed his mind about that, but we both became teachers instead. He taught English and I taught math. And we had three beautiful children. I stopped working for a long time, till all the kids were in elementary school. I missed working, but the kids were a lot of fun.

He thought I was pretty when I'd go out. I'd always live up to that. And I thought he was handsome. I didn't have much jealousy 'cause he was just such a sweet person. I can't remember no hard arguments like young people had. I can't even imagine what our arguments would be about. I guess other girls. He was a high school teacher, so he came in contact with a lot of young ladies. But I was always his prom night date. That would be my test: to keep myself together for prom night. My hairdresser always knew when I was going to prom. I would start off with my own long hair and got it all done up for the day.

He would love to show me off. We danced the first dance and the last dance. We had a lot of fun.

The ladies and I had a club down south. I can't remember the name of it now. But we'd get together and have a meeting once a month. We'd have refreshments and talk about life, you know. And once a year we'd have a dance. The fellas would come and see what we'd been up to. We'd have a band and wear the same color dresses. Boy, I missed that when I came up north. I tried to have a club when we moved, but nobody up here was ready for it.

Emmitt made me be self-sufficient. He could type and write so well. He could do a lot of things so when we first got married I thought he should do them for me too. If I had to type a paper, I'd want him to do it for me. I mean I _was_ his wife! But he would always make me do things for myself. He never would treat me inferior to him. He learnt me how to drive. A lot of men didn't want their wives driving, but he taught me how to do it so I could take care of myself.

After we had our children, and they were all in school, I began to teach math over in Georgia. And that was a big challenge.

Nobody around teaching math but the men and myself. But I did alright. I missed my family though. We were separated. My son and husband in Alabama and the girls and me in Georgia. I taught in Georgia for about four years and I would drive home on the weekends. I was actually driving home the evening of the march from Selma to Montgomery. They were throwing rocks and everything, but we made it okay because I had my kids with me.

I didn't have time to march in the riots. I was too busy teaching. I approved of it but I just didn't have time to be a part of it. Some of those people that were walking, they didn't have jobs. I had to keep my job, you know?

We moved to Detroit in 1967. The same year as the riot. We came up here because I hadn't been able to get a job in Montgomery. But I would have stayed in Montgomery, even with all the stuff going on. Yes, I believe I would have stayed. Alabama was home. I liked it. We had a lot of fun down there. I guess it was a chance for my kids to have a better education up here, but we had good schools down there too. My son was anxious to come up here though, 'cause he was the oldest. He was fifteen. But I came to Detroit mostly to connect the family together. I didn't want us to be apart the whole week.

I didn't really ride the bus much because we had a car. But if you messed up and sat in the front of the bus, wasn't nobody gonna bother you much. It wasn't as bad as some people make it. I mean, it is bad sitting in the back and I disagree, but I never came in contact with all that. Though it was uncomfortable, I'm sure, to those people who worked every day and had to ride the bus.

Moving up here wasn't easy. This was a completely different town you know. And then I had to get used to teaching in a different situation and whatnot. But it was okay because I had more education than anyone at my school so I didn't have no inferiority complex. *My college taught us well, so I did okay. I didn't have no trouble at all. I didn't even realize that I was being observed as I taught for two years. I had a very good principal. I guess I must've impressed him. When I was done being observed, he came in and sat in my chair at my desk and said, "Mrs. Bowen, you're off probation. You made it okay. You did beautiful." So that was done and I stayed at that school till I retired. I had good coworkers…not all good you know…because I was from the south and maybe my language might've been a little different than theirs, so they treated me a little differently. Where I was from, we'd all say "hello" and "good morning." We'd all speak to each other in the morning back down south. But up in the northern state they'd walk by and act like they didn't see you sometimes, so I had to get used to that. But I learned how to do that too eventually, so it wasn't too bad. And I had family up here so that helped too. My sisters and my brother and whatnot. It was alright.*

They loved Emmitt a lot here in the city. Being a Prisoner of War, he was written up in the local papers. He'd come into the city and talk and teach. But he still never talked to me about his time over there. I guess I learned patience from that. When you get married you usually learn how to communicate, but he didn't really. Or not as well as I did. I don't know, I guess what he had been through and all that…it affects you, you know. That kept him holding back.

But I had a pretty full life and he did too. I would think it was the best life for me. I don't know no other way it could've gone that would've been better. I did enjoy my life and I'm still enjoying it. Some of the younger people on my street ask me questions about how to get along with their boyfriends and so on. I try to give them the best advice I can. Some of them aren't married and I listen at 'em and I don't think some of 'em will ever marry. But they a lot of fun.

So that's that. I still miss him a lot. I never found no other partner that I enjoyed just talking with. My son said, "If you ever find somebody else you want to talk to, you should…"

But I never did.

ANNA BOWEN

THE ART OF JOGGING

Kathy, 51

Tom, 65

married 3 years

Kathy and Tom live in a bright airy house right across the street from "Mushroom Park." In the sixties, someone thought it was a swell idea to build tall cement structures in the shape of mushrooms for kids to climb on. The only problem is, these structures are extremely difficult to climb and are, in fact, pretty dangerous. A source of constant worry for parents and the cause of cuts, bruises, sprained ankles and broken bones to countless children. Yet, after all these years, no one has ever removed them. They stand tall.

I'm Kathy and I'm fifty-one.

I'm Tom and I'm sixty-five. And we've been married for three years. We were neighbors. Kathy moved in across the street in 2001.

And around 2004 we started running together.

So we were neighbors and friends and joggers. I think the jogging led us to miles and miles of talking and getting to know one another. We would use that time to work through all the different things that we were going through personally.

We really became drawn to one another because of all the talking we did. Quite often we would run early in the morning and if one of us couldn't make it we would come over with a note or something. It became more and more regular. If we didn't do it, because of weather or injury or whatever, we really missed it. It was pretty significant to miss that time.

I think we were running a couple of times a week.

And we established a route that was probably five or six miles, so that kept us engaged.

I just started looking more and more forward to running with her. Then there was an art exhibit going on with Chihuly, a guy who does glass blowing. When I first heard about glass blowing I thought about a vase or an ashtray. Chihuly's stuff is ceiling to floor. They're stunning. So I was really taken by the work and asked Kathy if she wanted to go up to the Institute of Art with me. This was in Late December of 2004. I think that was the first time we did something that wasn't related to running.

Even at that time it wasn't truly a date. We were joggers going out of our jogging element and doing something that we were both interested in. We had both come from long marriages. I had been married for twenty years and Tom had been married for twenty-six when we met.

I think we were very cautious and sensitive about each other's lives and situations and ex's and all of that. So dating was a gradual process.

Another thing that happened during that early dating time was my sister and my nephew sort of landed on my lap. They were coming from a horrible separation between my sister and her now ex-husband, so they moved into my house and I was taking care of them. I think that situation also slowed us down and kept our "dates" to jogging, art and meals together. There was no pressure to "move forward" or move in with one another. We took our time.

I think it was great to slow things down. It kept things in more of a conversation mode. Conversation became a big part of spending time together.

We also started making meals together two to three times a week. I'm the salad person and he's the griller.

During those meals we were at the table, I'd say two and a half to three hours at least. I think that was a real significant piece in terms of getting to know each other.

I remember how we used to just sit there for hours and tell each other stories. Tom has lots of people stories and I have lots of teaching stories. We really listen to each other. That was really a big part of our courtship. Tom has an incredible art of seeing the "big picture" about someone's life. A well-trained psychologist does that I think, but he brought that to our relationship. I really cherished all those meals.

After a while we began to talk about marriage. We each had our own, very separate lives so the blending of all our stuff was going to be an issue. We eventually decided to bring in a third party and talk to a counselor to help us decide if we should get married or not.

Tom is fifteen years older than me and has a son who is in his twenties so that was going to be different. And me living with my sister and nephew caused some complications as well, so we decided to talk to someone about everything going on in our lives and prep for the possibility of engagement and marriage. And we still see her from time to time. That has been extremely valuable to us to have another person we can check in with.

We also talked with a budget counselor a couple of times about how to integrate our households. That helped us make some decisions about housing as we were moving towards getting married.

So Tom had it planned out that we were going to take a weekend in Chicago for July 4th and see "Cirque du Soleil." I had been once before in Florida and I talked about it all the time. Of course, I didn't know there were going to be other surprises for that weekend. I thought the tickets were big enough. But he was carrying around the ring the whole time.

I had talked to Kathy's parents before that weekend.

Right. He did the good permission thing, which my dad loved. Even at our age!

Well it's kind of a tradition I guess.

Then we went into wedding planning mode and made a plan to get married a year later. That next year was so exciting to us because we wanted everything to be handmade, artistic and creative.

Our style. And that took a lot of work.

We found a minister based out of a Unitarian church in Chicago. So we started to meet up with her and she sort of became a counselor for us too.

She helped us design our wedding and we got to really plan everything the way we wanted. She had a lot of ideas and it felt like everything was aligned.

It really did. The people we were connected to were not only invited to the wedding, but were participating in it, so that made it very special and very unique.

We wrote our own vows. We spent a lot of time on those, going through them and editing. We used quotes from books and poems. It all felt really good to us.

It was very unique, very unusual.

Tom and I created a dance, which was sort of symbolic, about the life cycle and we made these scarves for people to use. We were all on an open rooftop, in bare feet, dancing. And even that day I remember standing back and going, we designed this! You know? This all came from our imagination. All of the planning, from the flowers to the tablecloths, we did it together…I mean I do like doing those things, but Tom was on board with everything.

Getting married to Kathy differed from my previous wedding and marriage tremendously. The ceremony itself revealed two people who were creating an experience <u>together</u>. Two people who were ready to spend their lives together. I didn't think about partnership when I got married before in the same way as I did when I married Kathy.

I think from all our talking prior to the wedding and opening up in counseling, we really became exposed and vulnerable with one another. We were willing to talk about who we were and willing to talk about our previous marriages. Earlier in my life I wouldn't have been willing to open up so much.

When you're twenty or twenty-five, what you're looking for in a partner is a lot different than when you're in your fifties and sixties. The types of superficial things that used to matter don't really matter anymore. It's who that person is inside: The integrity they have and the love they have for your family and friends and for you.

Through my work I've met some women in their twenties and thirties who have made decisions to cut off weddings and engagements in order to explore themselves and who they are. I think that it is so brilliant to tune in and realize that you are really giving yourself a gift when you explore yourself and travel and meet people.

I think a virus takes hold when you're in your twenties. The big question becomes, "Where am I going, and who am I going with?" People attempt to answer those questions about career and long-term relationships in that period of time, so I think there's a real push for people to couple at that time. The career piece especially compels people to only look externally. I think once you are more established in a career it's easier to be reflective internally about what's going on with what you want. And when you allow yourself to reflect on that, you learn a lot about yourself and the type of relationships you want in your life.

I think of other people I know that got married so young, the way I did. There's this sense of falling in love and families meeting each other and liking each other. Then there's the idea of the *"perfect" house and job and children. But that early on in life, you can't get to the core of <u>who</u> someone is. All of that other stuff is so external. And maybe it's only natural that young people are not willing to explore their core first. Tom and I often say we met at the right time. We were ready to dive in.*

FILL IN THE GAPS

Peter, 29

David, 30

married 2 years

As I knock on the door of Peter and David's apartment, I am immediately met by the sound of high-pitched barking. Peter pokes his head outside. "I should've asked you if you're okay with dogs," he says. "They're crazy and jumpy and they will lick you." "Oh that's okay" I whisper, "I love dogs." The high-pitched yapping continues non-stop as I begin to set up my equipment. "But don't you guys have kids? Will the barking wake them up? It's only 8:30." "Oh that's one of the good things about them." Peter says, "They go to sleep at 8 and are out till the next day. They can sleep through anything. They had to sleep through much worse before they came our way…"

My name is Peter and I am twenty-nine.

My name is David and I am thirty. And we've been together for...

Eight years.

Eight and a half years.

Eight and a half years. I feel like I'm in the middle of "When Harry Met Sally."

I feel like I'm back in therapy.

We've been married for two years. And we both tell the story of how we met differently. Do you want to tell it?

How about I tell and you correct it.

Okay.

Peter and I both went to NYU and we had mutual friends. One of our friends had written a show that Peter was in, and I went to go see it. I wasn't an actor, but I was interested in it and I wanted to show my support. The show wasn't that great.

We had dead babies on the stage. It was "art."

But I was totally head over heels for him. And I'm not like that. I'm not a very visually oriented person and I don't usually care about things like that.

Slash everyone he's dated is a gorgeous super model.

Well, maybe gorgeous super models have a thing for me.

Okay.

In any event I was really into him and I saw him in the lobby after the show. He was talking to a friend of mine so I went up to them and I introduced myself. And after he left I asked my friend for his number. Then a couple of days later I called him up and asked him out. Okay Peter, fix it.

There's no real "fixing." I'm just more detail oriented. The night that I met him I was with my ex-boyfriend…

Who was not an ex at the time.

I was meeting his mom for the first time. And I was not talking to our friend, David was. I walked up to them and he was wearing a baseball cap, which he doesn't remember, and I was wearing really ugly boots. I thought that he was incredibly attractive. We sort of flirted while I was standing five feet away from my ex-boyfriend's mother. It was kind of sad. But the next day at school my friend and I acted like schoolgirls. She was like, "David thinks you're really cute!" and I was like, "I think he's really cute, give him my number okay?" And she was like, "Well, shouldn't you be the man and just do it yourself?" And I was like, "No, you do it."

Wait, wait, wait, I asked her for your number! And I also walked up to you guys. I'm sorry if you remember it differently but that's the way it happened.

Well in either case, we went out on our first date and I, three days later, broke up with my boyfriend and six months later, David broke up with his.

Okay, let's be clear. Peter's boyfriend at the time was all of three feet away. Mine was three thousand miles away and we hadn't spoken in over six weeks. The relationship was over. Peter just likes to make himself feel better.

So on our first date we went to dinner and a show. We're theatre people, sorry.

Anyway, we went to dinner and I famously told him that I was a Jewish vegetarian and then I ordered a burger with bacon. I thought that would be a hysterical thing to say. Sometimes I have a really perverse sense of humor. But Peter didn't know what to do with that. I am not Jewish nor am I a vegetarian.

It was clear that this date wasn't going to go well when this happened. I was like, "Who is this? And what is this joke? It's not even funny." Then we got to the play and I was like, this is the worst first date ever!

We went to see a show all about a first date gone wrong. It started out okay and then it became a stalking situation and then there was violence. It was a thriller I guess. I thought the play was actually okay. But apparently I leaned over to him in the middle of the play and said something goofy like...

"I guess we're doing a little bit better than this." And that's when I was like, "Okay he's funny. He's an okay guy." Then afterwards we had a second dinner. It was a reboot. And at the end of the date he did this weird bow thing. I think he didn't want to leave and was feeling awkward, so he bowed. Then he walked away down the subway. And as he left I was like, "I'm not sure...but I think I like him!" I will always remember the bow thing as the moment where David became incredibly charming because it was so awkward and funny at the same time. Then on our second date we went to Prospect Park in Brooklyn and we both had to use the

bathroom. And I'll never forget this. David said to me, "You know, the most awkward thing about being on a date as a gay man is that you have to go to the bathroom together."

You don't get that break on a date! <u>And</u> you're typically in the next urinal! Is that weird to anyone else but me? I always found it incredibly awkward.

David was the man of the funny one-liners. But I wasn't sure they were funny at first.

He hadn't gotten used to my sense of humor.

Nope. But I was sold on him when he bowed.

I was sold on Peter when I first laid eyes on him. And I don't even know why. I have never had an experience like that. I have never been drawn to someone like that. It has caused a lot of heartbreak since…and joy.

We moved in together pretty quickly after we started dating. It was pretty much three months after we had exchanged names.

There were financial considerations as to why it happened the way it happened. Everything was changing at that time. We both had just graduated from college…it was basically a fling-y thing to do. Then when we got domestically partnered it was pretty unromantic as well. A friend of ours at the time had gotten cancer and he was uninsured. It was just one of those awful situations. Peter was also uninsured at the time and I had insurance because I was a schoolteacher. So I told him, "Peter, we're going to go down to city hall and we're going to get domestically partnered so you can be on my insurance." It wasn't romantic at all.

It was kind of romantic until we got there. Then when we got there it was just a sad DMV room with girls in wedding dresses and pigeons pooping everywhere. It wasn't what I wanted it to be. Then we were charged an extra dollar because we were gay…it just felt kind of bizarre.

It was a form, a stamp, a cashier's check and a "Next!" I knew that going in, but it was disappointing for Peter. That was in 2006.

But we always knew we were going to get married eventually.

Proposal is a deeply radical thing for a gay couple. It's not like the obvious next step. When we first started dating, gay marriage didn't really exist in the United States, so I assumed it would be many decades before the politics would change. But then over the course of our relationship, gay marriage became a reality. In 2008, gay marriage became legal in California. So we rushed towards the idea of getting married there. We set a date and picked a venue…and then Prop 8 happened. So we called the venue and cancelled. Tucked our tails between our legs and moved on.

The real tuck between the legs happened when we called to cancel our venue. They had not actually reserved the venue for us because we were gay. That was a really sad moment. But relatively soon thereafter we went to Guatemala on a vacation together. We were hiking up this volcano, which was one of the greatest moments of my life, and we decided in that moment that we were going to give New York a chance. We were going to see if they were going to make it legal or not and then we were going to get married regardless, wherever it would have to happen. It was at that moment where we decided we wanted to buy our engagement rings while we were in Guatemala.

On that hike we met this woman. Her brother was a silver smith. She gave us his card and said, "I'll take you!"

And David was like, "No, we can find it." So we got lost in the Guatemalan jungle, trying to get to this silver smith's house.

It was Guatemalan <u>suburbia</u>. It was a mile from our hotel. It was not that big of a deal.

Well, a mile is far! So we landed in this deserted area and went up to this old man. David asked him if he knew where this silver smith's house was and this guy was like, "Well, that's his mom over there." So we followed this woman on a scooter to this little shack. While we were there we looked at these rings that had two vines coming together. They had been handmade, they matched, and there were only two of them. It was very clear that these were going to be our engagement rings. We ended up spending a couple of hours there while he resized them for us. Then on the way back, it was really hot, and my finger started to swell. I couldn't get the ring off! I remember saying, "This is not good! This is a bad sign!" But then we got back to the hotel room and we were so happy and giddy. Even though there was no "real" proposal, we were happily giddy that this was finally happening. When we got home, New York fell through so we decided to get married in New Hampshire.

At that time there were five states where we could legally get married. Now there are eight.

But everything's flipping back and forth. It's all a mess.

We weren't sure how many people were going to come. We told the venue that maybe twenty-five people would show up. There ended up being a hundred and ten people at this wedding. <u>Everyone</u> came. And let's be clear, it was an eight-hour subway, train, bus, and shuttle ride to get there.

Our wedding was the proudest achievement of my life.

We had this crazy idea that it could somehow be this wholesome Mormon family reunion...

Because David's whole family is Mormon...

And also like a bohemian sex party at the same time...and we kind of pulled it off! My family is a crazy, crazy mix of the supportive and absurd. The vast majority of them showed up, and they were marvelous. And the vast majority of them voted the other way come Election Day. It's this funny back and forth.

More of his family showed up than mine.

That's the funky thing about Mormons. You've never met more kind, caring, considerate people and coupled with that is an absolute loyalty to the marching orders of the prophet. Whatever the prophet says, you do it, and you smile, and then you go back to being as kind and caring as you can possibly be. That struggle remains and will remain for a very long time.

The wedding was dry but in our cabin there were bins and bins and bins of beer. We put all of our crazy, artsy friends together in a big barn and after our rehearsal dinner we had a game night and got really drunk.

Then we went skinny-dipping. And the next night we had a giant campfire and our friend who introduced us, and has remained a very good friend of ours, began a sort of ceremony. We got up, bawled our eyes out, and when it was all said and done we were married!

Everyone was a part of the wedding. We had friends singing and reading poetry. It was great.

Peter's uncle showed up dressed in Little Bo Peep drag and sang a song for us while accompanying himself on the accordion.

It. Was. Brilliant.

Everyone took part in this community event. We had assumed people wouldn't really take part in it, but it was just <u>joy</u> the whole weekend.

And I wore a kilt, which was fun. I'm a mutt but I claim to be Scottish.

Then after a year or so, we decided to move out to California and settle down.

A huge part of the reason we moved out to the west coast was to be closer to David's family so we could have grandparents for our kids.

We are fostering two kids together now. We started training for foster parenting and within two months we had kids. We started on this process about two years ago and then we realized that we didn't really have the support network we needed out in New York. It would've been us against the world.

So we moved out here and sort of dove in. It was <u>way</u> too quick. I think if it had not been so quick I probably would've woken up and been like, what are we doing? This was in May.

Four months ago. They're seven and eleven. Although they were six and ten when they came to us. They've had birthdays.

It's like life on fast forward.

If you think about it, we have an eleven-year-old son, which means Peter would've been eighteen when he was born.

Well it's sad because his actual parents were fifteen. But they're really good kids. I mean, they're insane and it's really difficult dealing with their mom, but they're good kids. To be a foster parent you can be certified either with the state or with agencies. We are certified with an agency. We trained through them and everything.

But it's not an adoption agency like most people think. It's a foster care agency that contracts with the government to prepare and support foster parents.

There are way too many children in the system and there's no way a government agency could keep track or take care of all of these kids, so they contract with various agencies. Anyway, we trained though them and immediately started getting phone calls when we were done.

I wanted a thirteen or fourteen year old.

I thought I wanted a baby. And let me tell you, I'm glad we don't have one because I would not have any idea what to do with one.

We thought we were going to get a single child to start off with.

I don't know how it happened, but at some point we were just like, "We're getting siblings." I thought that was great because David could get an older kid and I could have a younger kid. But as I said before, if I had stopped and thought about it, I would've pulled out. I had no idea what I was getting into.

Well, Peter was the youngest child in his family and had no experience in child care. Whereas I was the oldest child from a gargantuan family and I had spent eight years as an educator. I had a lot of experience and knowledge and to some extent I knew what to expect. I don't think Peter really did.

I didn't. It has been a huge learning process. About two weeks in I was ready to bail.

And I smacked him down really hard. Gave him a reality check.

I mean it's the most difficult thing I've ever done in my life. And I know a lot of parent's say that but honestly this is the most difficult thing I have ever done in my life. My daily mantra is, "I am smarter than a seven-year-old...I am smarter than a seven-year-old..." And our eleven-year-old came home two weeks after we got him with a pamphlet that said, "Your Body and You." Basically, "Semen and You." And I was like, "Wow. I'm having a sex conversation with my eleven-year-old who I just met two weeks ago!"

I came home that night and Peter said, "You need to have a talk with your son." And he handed me the pamphlet.

I did the first pass but I needed help.

On some level, having kids has changed our relationship. I think it generally has made us a better couple. The major thing it's done for me is that I put up with Peter's bullshit less. I tend to call him earlier when he's not doing his best because all of a sudden it's no longer the stakes of me and us, but of the kids as well.

The stakes are multiplied by a million. You throw two children in the mix and the stakes are going to be raised.

These are <u>very</u> difficult kids. They're both behind academically and our youngest boy is very difficult to parent. He has a lot of the characteristics of an autistic kid and he's just really nasty a lot of the time.

But he's just enough mainstream that the nasty doesn't quite make any logical sense. For some reason it always surprises me. It's like, "Oh! Okay, we're in a bad mood today." This kid can be skipping down my hallway and then all of a sudden he tears a painting off my wall and throws it across the room.

First of all, when you're a foster parent, you don't get any information. When the kids come you get a phone call saying, "I've got these kids, their names are, their ages are…do you want them?"

The day after we were certified we got a phone call and I was like, "I'm not ready, sorry!" And then she called the next day and we were like, "No, not yet." And then the next day she called <u>again</u> and I was like, "Hold up. Are you gonna call me every day until I take some kids?" And she said, "Yup."

That's an indication of how great the need actually is. And so Peter and I said, "Okay, call us next Wednesday." So we got ourselves together and the next Wednesday they called us about these boys. When she called she said, "We don't know if they speak English, they seem to be Hispanic. They're incredibly skinny, malnourished and underfed. And they're incredibly filthy."

When they arrived here they hadn't bathed in three weeks. But they spoke English just fine. Actually, they don't know Spanish at all. And our eldest is incredibly overweight. He's pretty much the opposite of malnourished. The misinformation is amazing.

So they showed up and each had a piece of paper with their name on it. They had no clothes other than the ones they had been wearing for the last three weeks. The first thing we did was we went to Target and bought them three outfits each.

We were completely unprepared to know sizes. We just had no idea. We got Gabe, our eleven-year-old, a youth large…

He was walking around like a Chelsea boy, with his stomach poking out. It was hysterical.

The clothes we bought him that night, our seven-year-old now wears. We had absolutely no idea what we were doing.

And also, you have certain things that you're supposed to do. For example, you're supposed to see a doctor within the first seventy-two hours and they're supposed to be in school the next day. But there's no way that can happen! How are you supposed to enroll your kids in a school? Well, you have to find the local neighborhood schools and see if they have space for you. Well, these are special education kids. Well, we don't take kids like that at this school. Four schools later, phone calls to assistant principals, the insurance isn't going through…it's now the weekend…and that first weekend Peter was gone on a business trip.

David was here holding down the fort. He took the boys to Old Navy and Antonio ran out of the store and started eating dirt out of a planter.

For the first couple of days Antonio was basically non-verbal. He just moaned.

They were both severely neglected. Their parents did not talk to them and the only way they got any kind of attention was acting out severely.

When we took them to Target that first night, Antonio spent most of the evening hiding under the clothes racks.

But they've made huge strides.

Gabe has gone from not knowing how to subtract four from seven to working on fractions and doing grade level math at the moment. Antonio's mental disability is much more severe.

He actually has a cognitive delay of some kind.

He probably will never operate on grade level, but his behavior has improved significantly and his social skills have improved in a huge way.

They are wonderful boys. We have huge successes with them and then we have major setbacks. Last week we had a huge success and yesterday was a failure on my part. Today I had a huge success with Gabe and a failure with Antonio. But these are our kids, you know? It's like we had them. No, they're not biologically our children, but they are absolutely a combination of the two of us.

Of course there's a ton of uncertainty here. We have no idea what the future brings. Their parents are still very much in the system and are actively, if inconsistently, trying to get them back, so there's a pretty good chance that a few months from now they will indeed be going back to mom and dad.

We'll know for sure in February.

Well, we'll have more information but we won't know for sure.

I like saying we'll know for sure, even though we won't know anything.

The system treats foster parents like…

Parasites.

Not like parasites. Like worker bees. You are a worker for hire. They pay you. I mean they pay you six hundred bucks a month, but they pay you. And for a lot of people that's enough to live off of. But they tell you nothing. And you have no rights when it comes to the courts or access to information or documents.

I took Gabe to Sylvan Learning Center today and they asked me, "Who are you?" Obviously I have this Mexican boy with me and clearly I'm not his dad, so I have to just claim to be his dad, otherwise I don't really have the right to talk to them about my child.

We don't have any rights to make any sort of educational decisions for these kids.

Everything has to be cleared through mom who is incredibly difficult to find and doesn't really care and who has no interest in education to begin with. But every day is a learning process. It's about waking up the next day and making better choices and affirming for one another that we have one another's best interests at heart.

It's also about gratitude and perspective. And the good thing is, now that we have kids we don't have time to get into stupid fights!

I think we used to fight sometimes because we were bored. And there's no time to be bored anymore. Mostly when we're together, it's just about being together. And when we do fight I think the stakes are more real. We used to fight a lot about nothing and those fights would usually escalate and get out of hand. There was one time when we were both naked, running down the block and screaming at one another…

There have been several "naked running down the's…"

We can be a little dramatic at times. But we don't fight about trivial things anymore. Although the fact that we fight about "real things" now is painful.

Early on in our relationship Peter thought that any fighting was a sign of something awful. I came from a family where fighting was a normal thing that you did without disastrous stakes. It was just something that happened and it was almost a loving act in a way. As a result, I'm very hypercritical.

It's impossible to live with him.

I have stupidly high standards about everything.

And I'm a people pleaser so I desperately want to please him and meet his standards. I think early on in our relationship it meant so much to me to be the person he wanted me to be, but now I think I have more perspective to know what I should care about and what I shouldn't care about.

And now I know what to actually be critical about and what to let go.

Our relationship has changed more than I ever thought it

would. When we first started dating I had no idea what I was getting into. In many ways I assumed it would be this idyllic, love-y dove-y thing. I thought that everything was going to be hunky dory in this cookie cutter world. David started dating when he was fourteen but I had only been dating for a year when we met. I had absolutely no idea what to expect out of a gay relationship. I just assumed we were going to be the gay version of Mary Tyler Moore and Dick Van Dyke (I was raised by Nick at Nite) so when that didn't happen, my little picture frame burst. It took a long time for it to burst, but it did. Sexually, David and I weren't compatible in a lot of ways. David asked me at one point to open up our relationship sexually and that was a huge issue for me.

It took us years to work through.

We struggled sexually, but we worked so well in so many other capacities that we knew we wanted to save what we had.

We eventually tried to open our relationship and it has ultimately worked out for the best. But it was really rocky for a long time.

Our relationship has had huge ups and downs.

They're always bigger for Peter than they are for me.

Well, I'm a more emotional person. But I just love being around David. It is the thing that I most look forward to. It's stupid, but I always think about how much I love going to Costco with him. I just enjoy doing those domestic, silly things. I enjoy building a life with him.

I agree. I remain floored by Peter's beauty. And I don't just mean his physical beauty, although I certainly mean that too, but multiple times every day I take in that shocking moment of encountering him.

I think we both started out as kids for sure and we both had this idea of what our relationship would be like. Many times over we have shattered that picture and then reset it. But in some ways I still feel very much like the kid in the ugly boots who met him in the lobby of the theatre building.

We actually are a really good team.

We fill in the gaps in many ways for one another. A lot of my strengths are his weaknesses and a lot of his strengths are my weaknesses in that cliché way. Ultimately at the end of the day, after I got over all of my "ideas" of what this relationship would be, I really felt secure in what I saw us building. And I really do honestly believe that David challenges me to be a better person. I enjoy who I am with him and I enjoy that I am able to challenge him as well.

I love that Peter continues to be impressed by me and over me all at the same time.

I think we both agree that we've made the choice to be together. There are times when it sucks but at the end of the day it never really sucks because he is my best friend and I get so much gratification from seeing him grow and seeing us grow together.

There was a period during our relationship where Peter kept asking me, "Why are we together? Why are you with me?" And I don't really have an answer to that question. I hate that. I usually have answers for everything. The answers tend to be sort of textbook and I pride myself on being knowledgeable about all sorts of things. It's a source of comfort for me. And maybe part of what I value about my relationship with Peter is <u>not</u> having an answer for that question. When I saw him in that horrible show and just sort of knew how I felt about him, well, that level of mysticism is not really a "me" thing. Maybe that's part of the draw of our relationship and why I come back to Peter over and over again. I don't really know <u>why</u> I'm with him, I just know I want to be. Is that lame and unsettling?

No.

I also have little pat answers like, he likes to be tickled. What adult man likes to be tickled? And he's really, really talented in the kitchen, in the bedroom, as a parent, as a tutor, as an intellect, and as a performer. I have plenty of reasons why we <u>shouldn't</u> work and yet somehow in spite of all that I don't really consider the other option. It's just not an option.

It's not an option.

FROM SCRATCH

Brenda, 65

Deren, 64

married 42 years

I arrive about an hour early for my appointment with Brenda and Deren. I suppose I am just a little too eager to get started. Deren has just come in from a bike ride and Brenda is cooking lunch. "I can come back in an hour if you'd prefer," I say. But they won't hear of it. Instead, I eat lunch with them and chat a little bit. Their beautiful, spacious home, which they have refurbished and decorated themselves, is three stories tall with high ceilings and old wooden floors. Everything in their house has been purchased while traveling or is homemade. While we eat Brenda says to me, "I don't know what you're planning on getting from this interview…Deren and I really don't have much to say. We're pretty old and boring."

I'm Brenda, I'm sixty-five and I've been married for forty-two and a half years.

I'm Deren and I'm quite young at sixty-four, and I've been married for those same forty-two and a half years. We met on the Diag at the University of Michigan in 1965. It was our freshman year. I was studying engineering at the time. I hadn't declared any specialty yet, and Brenda was in the liberal arts school.

Yup. I thought I was going to be a foreign correspondent. Turned out to be a speech pathologist. Darn.

I was out walking with a friend who lived in my dorm, he had actually gone to high school with Brenda, and he introduced us.

I think I was by myself. I just walked by these guys who were extremely intoxicated because it was some sort of fraternity rush thing, and this guy I had known in high school, who had barely spoken to me before, acted like I was his long, lost friend. He's a great guy. He was in our wedding.

And I must've remembered this meeting because I got her number and called her up. I wasn't <u>that</u> drunk.

Then we went out on our first date. Which was awful. It was absolutely the worst thing you could possibly do on a first date. We went to the movie theatre and saw this horribly depressing film called "The Pawnbroker." You do <u>not</u> want to see it. It is so painful. There are all of these horrible images of the holocaust. It's just awful! One of the most terrifying scenes is when this man smashes his hand down on one of those spikes that you put receipts on. I was just bawling by the time this movie was over. It was too intense and emotional. It was certainly not a first date kind of movie…but it was what was playing at the movie theatre on South U (university) *and State Street.*

Then we went and got a lemonade at "The Brown Jug."

And we shared a grilled cheese sandwich! Which is very significant because now we're back to the sharing sandwiches thing. We're at the age now where we're not eating too much and so we share. Although we were probably doing it then because we didn't have enough money for a whole sandwich each. Well, I certainly didn't.

I didn't either.

But then, <u>long</u> periods of time would pass and Deren wouldn't call! And in those days girls did NOT call guys. That was just a complete and utter no-no. So you were sitting there…waiting for something to happen. It was terrible.

I don't remember not calling!

Oh yes. Long times would pass and he wouldn't call, and then he'd call and eventually we were going out every Friday. We had these nice Friday dates.

At noon. Friday at noon.

It took a while for that to get going, but Deren was pretty much my only boyfriend. I had one boyfriend in high school and one boyfriend in college. And that was that!

So in '65 we met and in '69 we were married. It was kind of a low-key affair. As I recall we just sat down, discussed it and decided, "Well, yeah, I guess we should get married."

The 60's were awful for anything like that. It just wasn't a romantic time. It was a time of sort of rejecting everything that we thought the establishment expected us to do. So I guess we thought we were very mature doing it this way. We went to some bar…what was it. The Village something.

"The Village Bell."

"The Village Bell." And we had a beer. Exams were over and that was where we sort of officially decided that we were going to get married. But before that, we had decided to join the Peace Corps together, so we kind of just evolved into this agreement that we were going to be together. We went looking for a ring and this one stuck out to me. I couldn't read the price, but I thought it was ten thousand dollars or something. It was in the window of this jewelry shop on South U. Our world was kind of small back then. It was…

South U.

South U. And State Street. And that was about it. Then one day I went back to the jewelry store and found out that this ring was only a hundred and ten dollars! So we bought it and that was my wedding ring. I loved that ring. It lasted twenty-five years. We put a lot of work into it, refinishing it and so on, but then it got retired.

So we got married and six months later we were in Ghana with the Peace Corps.

That was interesting to do right after we were married. We realized that about two thirds of the married couples we knew in the Peace Corps got divorced. We figured if we made it through those three years, we probably could make it through anything. I mean, it put a certain strain on your relationship to be uprooted from your culture, your family and your stuff and just be in a completely different world.

I can still remember my mom dropping us off at the airport. She cried.

I would've cried.

I think that was the only time I ever saw my mother cry.

She was very stoic, but she did cry. She didn't say, "Don't go." She just knew she wasn't going to be able to come and see us.

Nobody came to see us except one friend.

I think if our kids were to do that now, we would've gone. But back then, forty years ago, it was a bigger deal. And my parents, let's see, I think my dad was fine with it. Concerned. Like any father would be. But for the most part I think he felt like it was probably a good thing to do. But my mom wouldn't come and visit us because she was worried about bugs and snakes. She knew nothing about Africa. No one in our family knew anything about Africa. I don't think any of them could have named a single country.

We were in Ghana for three years in two different towns. The first town was the second largest town in Ghana and we decided that school was a little bit too fancy for us. There really wasn't a good Peace Corps experience to be had there.

Basically there were just way too many white people around. We didn't come thousands of miles to spend all this time with people who were just like us.

But there were other reasons why we left…

Oh yes. You see, we taught at a boarding school, so students were not allowed to go off campus. Well, some of the student body went off to town for some reason when they weren't supposed to. I don't know what they were doing. Getting into mischief I guess. So apparently this girl had run off to town and right outside my door a teacher was whipping her. She was screaming and crying. I went out there and said, "Please, stop. I'm trying to teach." This man was just completely offended and said I had no business telling him how to discipline his students. Finally I stood in front of him and said, "No. You're stopping. You're not doing this anymore. It's over. I'm teaching." And I sent this poor girl into my room.

Well! They did not take kindly to this at all. I got a little dressing down at the staff meeting and was told I didn't understand African children. I was told that I had no idea how to discipline these children and then I was asked to apologize. I said, "I have no apology." I didn't say anything else. I just sat there. Then I got just a tiny bit uppity and wrote letters to the teacher's colleges. I asked them what they were teaching about corporal punishment. I got two replies saying they no longer recommend corporal punishment. So I took that to the headmaster and I said, "Here you go. Stop hitting kids."

But it was very uncomfortable for me after that. Women were just supposed to sit quietly, keep their mouths shut and do what they were told. I had offended some of the teachers by doing what I did.

We met another volunteer, Vincent, who became a very good friend of ours during the Peace Corps training. We went to visit him several times in that first year and got to know his little town. Eventually we approached the headmaster of his school and said, "Hey, do you need a physics teacher and an English teacher?" And he said, "Actually, yeah we do." So we called up the Peace Corps and said, "We'd like to move so please send our check up here." And they did! So we moved.

We moved to a smaller town called Abetifi.

This school was a much simpler, poorer school and our house was made of mud and brick, with a cement courtyard that held the kitchen and the bathroom.

We never were thinking, "Oh we wish we had this, or we wish we had that…" Well, with the exception of running water. We really developed a great appreciation of running water and a constant awareness of the lack of it.

It wasn't so much the water itself, it was the pressure of the water. You would be amazed at just how much work that does for you.

But we had a really nice life. We had a woman and two children trying to wait on us and do all our housework. Even though this was a very poor school, the status of a teacher required a housekeeper in this culture. So when we moved to this house we were met by Auntie Grace and her two little girls, Abenaw and Adjua. Auntie Grace said that it was her job to take care of the Peace Corps. So, for thirty dollars a month, she would do all the cooking and the cleaning and the laundry. We said, "We can't have servants! We're Peace Corps Volunteers!" I mean you've got to be kidding. I've never in my life had a housekeeper! It was just too much of a social barrier for me to think of having a servant. So we proposed to Auntie Grace that we'd pay her the thirty dollars a month and she could live there and we could learn the language from her but we would do our own cooking and cleaning and so on. And she said, "Oh no Misses. This is not how we do it."

We eventually worked a compromise.

We did. I cooked. She cleaned. And we taught each other things. I learned to cook Ghanaian food from her and I taught her how to cook some things. We had a good time.

We had a great time. But even though we were having fun, we still had to figure out how to deal with Vietnam...

People were getting drafted all over the place. We had a friend who enlisted and was killed within six weeks so that had a sobering affect on us. It was just beyond comprehension why we were in this war. Was it worth somebody's life? Up until the time Deren was eligible for the draft, there were deferments for college and for all kinds of work. Then Nixon eliminated all deferments. Which was actually a good thing because that made it much more equal as far as the people in society who were going to suffer. So there was a lot more pressure to end the war. But for us it meant the Peace Corps wasn't going to be a deferment anymore. You could postpone your 1-A status but you were going to be in the lottery at some point. It's really complicated, but somehow the Peace Corps knew what numbers were going to be drawn. They told us, chances are they aren't going to draw any numbers higher than 150 this year, so request 1-A status. Deren's number was 173. So we did this, and Deren was in the lottery for one week in December of 1971. He didn't get drafted and then was no longer eligible, so we decided to stay in the Peace Corps for one extra year without the threat of the draft hanging over our heads.

Not only was it nice to be in the Peace Corps without that threat, but we thought we were doing good work. We were having a good time and we liked it.

We were only in our early twenties. When I think about the kids I know now, I ask myself, "What were we doing?"

We drove all over West Africa on a motorcycle. Went to all these different countries...we did a lot of crazy stuff!

I think there is a lot of luck in how things worked out for Deren and I because we were so young when we got married. I would never suggest to my kids that they get married at twenty-one and marry the second person they ever seriously dated. But, when I think back, very early on in our relationship Deren made this fantastic photo album for me and I knit him a couple of sweaters. I think there was something foretelling in that because we both like making things and working on projects. A lot of our relationship has been renovating our house together, building things and making stuff. We'd always start from scratch and do things the hard way. Well that was the view of our parents anyway. "Everything you do is so difficult! You could just go buy that!" But we never did. We tend to do everything from scratch. That's what the title of our book would be: "From Scratch." We both love it.

After we were done with the Peace Corps, we came back to Michigan. That year right after the Peace Corps was so much fun. We had gotten involved with Peace Corps recruiters and they would stay at our house.

It was pretty much an open house. Everybody would cook and play cards. We'd all go downtown and listen to music. People just slept in our living room and on the stairs and in the hallway...

We had the coolest house on the block. And we lived there for about six years before we had kids.

I think our parents wondered if we were ever going to have them. We don't have a very big family so they were eager for us to get started. But when we finally did have kids we were old enough. We were secure, we both had jobs, and we both agreed that the kids were the number one priority no matter what. There was none of this growing apart business. It seemed like people around us were divorcing a lot. We didn't have any reason to get divorced. I guess if I started beating him or something he'd have to divorce me. But seriously, I never wanted to put my kids through something like that. They needed to have a solid family. We had such a great time raising our kids and luckily we did fine. Our kids were such good kids.

We weren't really tested that much. We lucked out.

We were fortunate. The kinds of kids that I worked with for forty years, ones with disabilities and problems in their life, it puts stress on you that you can't imagine unless you've lived through it yourself. We were lucky. Our kids were healthy.

And they were good academically. We never had to push them to study or do their homework. They did it themselves.

When our daughter came home from college that first year she said, "You guys don't understand how different you are from most parents. I don't know if you're normal or what, but you wouldn't believe the stories I hear from my friends. Most parents just yell and fight." Then I tried to remember any arguments Darren and I ever had. I think I remember two.

I don't remember any…

One involved a time in our Volkswagen Beatle and it must've been 1970. He threw his hamburger to the floor of the car about something and neither of us can remember what it was. But I remember him throwing the hamburger!

Must've been a lousy hamburger.

Must've. But we really don't fight. We don't argue. Not that we agree on everything, but we don't disagree on things that are major. I think we've been good at handling stuff.

And we've handled some stuff. Family stuff…

The biggest thing for me was my mom had a mental health crisis. But it was preceded by thirty-five years of drinking and very hard times with her. So in the background of our great family life there was this looming problem. And it was always there. It would affect us intermittently. I would have her come visit and it would be another reminder that things were not okay. When I was pregnant with my son and things were completely out of control with mom, I used to make an appointment with myself that at four o'clock every day I would get home from work and cry for thirty minutes. Just sit in a chair and cry and get over it. I remember deciding that that was how I was going to cope with things. And then I thought to myself, "I am going to make this baby sick." I was just so full of anger and frustration. It was one of those situations that was so awful but no one could fix it.

Then I said to myself, "I am not going down with her ship. She is not going to affect my children." So we kept it out of our family life. Instead of saying, poor me, I have a mom who is out of control, I decided I wasn't going to get into that. I had to put my head down and plow through some really hard stuff. Thank goodness I had that moment of clear thinking. It wasn't an easy thing. But it is something that I look back on and think, wow…that could've had such a bad affect on my kids and my marriage. I'm so glad I didn't let myself go down the 'I feel sorry for myself' road. You have to live your own life.

We were naive. We thought it was just the alcohol but it ended up being severe mental illness.

But our daughter was about twelve and our son was fifteen before they knew anything about the problems with their grandmother. I never allowed it to affect them. It could've been a lot worse.

And now it is okay! She's fine and we're fine.

Once we knew that we were dealing with someone with a mental illness we said, "Let's fix this. We can make things better." And now we have our mom back. She's a doll.

That was a hard time but we helped each other through it. Brenda and I just really enjoy helping each other and being around each other. We don't <u>think</u> about spending the rest of our lives together, we just do it. We just keep making dinner and getting up in the morning.

Deren's a really good guy. He doesn't smoke, or drink…

I don't mess with other women…I guess that just means I'm an old guy!

We were lucky. We had great kids and we love each other. I would start today from the beginning and do it all over again if I had the chance. It was so much fun.

ANNA BOWEN

NERDING OUT

Elizabeth, 30

Jeremy, 31

married 3 years

Elizabeth and Jeremy live in a small apartment in North Hollywood with their dog, Fred. Movie posters from "The Lord of the Rings" decorate their walls and their huge lizard, Gorbash, (named after one of the dragons from the 1982 animated film "The Flight of Dragons") sits silently in their kitchen. Hundreds of DVD's surround the television set. Although I have not known Elizabeth and Jeremy long, we have become fast friends in the crazy city of Los Angeles.

I'm Elizabeth.

I'm Jeremy.

I'm thirty.

I'm thirty-one. Hey, we're doing good so far!

We have been together for about five and a half years. We have our three-year wedding anniversary in about two weeks.

A few years ago I was working in Anaheim, but I had taken some time off to travel.

I had just moved to Los Angeles from New York and while he was away traveling, I began to work in his office.

My first day back, Elizabeth walked right up to me and said, "Hi, Jeremy!"

Well, Jeremy was like a legend in the office. I kept hearing about him and everyone knew who he was...I just really wanted to meet him!

She was very enthusiastic.

So we started working together. We began carpooling to work and became best friends. And we were both seeing other people at that time so dating wasn't even really on our radar.

Well, I thought she was hot, but I was dating a couple of ladies.

And I was in a destructive relationship with a "man-boy."

It's weird, but from the time we met, I knew I was going to date Elizabeth someday. It made all the sense in the world to me. I knew that I was really attracted to her, I really liked her, she made me laugh and she was really smart. These were things that I had not had in the relationships of my past. So I knew I was going to date her eventually, but I had crap that I needed to work out first...

And I was with another guy.

The funny thing is, I never felt jealous of this guy. Ever. I was so confident that Elizabeth and I were going to be together that I never felt intimidated or threatened by him. In a way, I kind of felt sorry for him! I knew he was going to fall by the wayside...and then I would come in and swoop her up.

Jeremy and I were already so comfortable together. From the get-go we just always fit.

I've been with some really wonderful people who were boring as hell. I mean, they were really nice...but that was about it. But being around Elizabeth is just so much fun! She is someone who can make me laugh like no other...it really is amazing how well we fit.

We finish each other's sentences. We quote lines from movies and TV shows out of nowhere together.

We actually went to Comic-Con together on our first date.

Oh yeah!

That solidified it even more for me because I knew we could nerd out together! I could be completely nerdy with her!

And I could be nerdy with him!

So after we had been dating for a little over a year, Elizabeth was going on a business trip to New York for a week. She really wanted me to go with her but I told her I had a ton of work to do and couldn't leave. Then I immediately called her friend Melody and told her about my "surprise engagement plan."

So I showed up in New York and I was really sad because Jeremy and I had never been apart for very long…but I had to get myself together because Melody told me she had planned a business dinner with some of the executives of the company.

I arrived in New York a little while later and got ready to surprise Elizabeth at the restaurant. I was worried about being late but I was ahead of schedule in every possible way. I got to my hotel in no time.

So I went to the subway station and made my way downtown. I didn't know New York very well but I found the restaurant and texted Melody. I told her, "Okay, you walk out and I'll walk in." And I didn't see her walk out. So I sent another text. "Where <u>are</u> you?" She texted, "I walked out, I don't see you!" Eventually I went into the restaurant and I didn't see them at all!

She had changed the restaurant at the last minute and Jeremy hadn't seen the email.

Yup. So I was at the wrong restaurant. In fact, I was sixty blocks in the wrong direction. So, I had a small heart attack, and then I called Melody…"Melody? Stall!"

Cut to the restaurant. I'm sitting there and I'm like, "Why won't they let us order? Where are these executives we're supposed to be meeting?" And Melody's like, "Oh it's fine! I'm sure they'll be here soon! So…um…do you have 20/20 vision…?" Seriously, the questions she was asking were ridiculous. I was getting really annoyed.

Overlap that with me sprinting to the nearest subway station. I didn't have the foresight to hail a cab. I didn't think about that. I didn't know what I was doing! I barely knew where I was! So I got down to the subway station and all of the uptown trains were closed. I had to take a train to Brooklyn and then go across the platform to go back uptown. I was easily 45 minutes late. It was really embarrassing. When I finally made it to the restaurant I didn't even take time to get myself together. I just walked right up to the table and asked her if she'd marry me. I was sweaty and gross and I felt like I was going to pass out because I had never run that fast in my life.

When I saw him I screamed, "What the F--K?" in the middle of this crowded, fancy restaurant (little old ladies turned around and shook their heads disapprovingly)…but then I said, "Yeah, okay!" And everyone cheered.

So we were engaged for about another year, and then we got married.

Man, I hate weddings. People are always stuck at tables waiting for food when really everyone just wants to drink and dance. So our goal was to have lots of booze and lots of dancing. We wanted people to have fun. We had an open bar, and a buffet with mashed potato martinis…

It was just a big party. I still have people say to me, "That was the most fun I've ever had at a wedding."

We had a folk band play. My mom sang. Jeremy sang…

And then we went on our honeymoon. I wanted to go to New Zealand because I wanted to see Mordor (from "The Lord of the Rings"). Which, as it turns out, is not real.

We compromised on Australia. We got to hold koalas.

When Elizabeth and I see cute animals we both lose brain cells. So the entire trip we were like, "Koala! Wombat! Sea turtle! Yay!"

We went snorkeling in the beautiful, clear water. It was so awesome.

We both love being outdoors and we love camping. Actually camping was another reason I knew I wanted to spend my life with Elizabeth. I have been with women who were like, "Oh, you get so dirty. Bugs? Gross." But Elizabeth is game for anything.

So after our honeymoon we came back to Los Angeles and started our lives as a married couple! And you always hear that the first year of marriage is really hard, but that just wasn't true with us.

Maybe it's because we lived together first.

Yeah. I can't imagine marrying someone without living with them first. I mean Jeremy's my best pal and all, but it is really difficult to live with somebody else.

Living with Elizabeth has made me grow and change in so many ways. I held onto grudges a lot in my previous relationships and I am honestly surprised that I can get over things as easily as I do with Elizabeth. I think a lot of that has to do with the way we handle things when we're upset. We really make sure to talk things through and listen to one another.

I think a lot of fights escalate because people don't talk things through. Then everything sits inside of you and grows and festers. That's when those really wonderful fights happen, where you fight about fourteen things…

Yeah, "Remember four weeks ago when you said this? Or five nights ago when you did this? Well I'm mad about that, even though I never told you…so there!"

If you don't bring things up right away and talk them through it can get really bad.

Usually we can sense if something is wrong with the other person and most of the time it just turns into a discussion.

Which is good because sometimes you just need to check in!

Elizabeth and I have had fights, but I can count the really bad ones on one hand.

I think that's because we have so much respect for one another and we're so compatible.

We have such similar interests. That song, "Opposites Attract" by Paula Abdul? Yeah, that's bullshit.

We're just really nerdy in the same way. We love horror movies and history and comic books.

And we also appreciate the stuff that we don't necessarily share with one another. For example, if I'm watching a game on TV, she'll come downstairs and say, "How's the game going, honey?" And I know she doesn't care at all…but she still asks! It's really nice!

Appreciating each other's interests is key. For our first anniversary Jeremy got me tickets to see "Billy Eliot" the musical…and I got him tickets to WWE.

I'm from Texas…we like weird things.

Yeah, like guys beating each other up in panties.

I think the bottom line is Elizabeth is someone who makes me feel good about myself. Always. Even when there's something I need to work on or I need to change. She never says, "You suck. Why are you this way?" She always makes me feel proud to be me. Any type of criticism is constructive and helps me become a better person.

I have dated guys who made me feel like crap. Jeremy has never once made me feel bad about myself.

It's kind of weird how clear it was. As soon as we started dating I was like, "Yup, this is it."

You have a list of things that you want out of a partner. Maybe its not formally written down, but it's there. And Elizabeth had them all.

It was very clear from the moment we started dating. We told each other that we loved each other pretty early on. We moved in together a few months later. And it never felt weird. It never felt rushed. It was just like, "Well we're going to be together for forever anyway, so we might as well get a move on."

And we know there will be challenges along the way. We're just getting started. We have a long way to go. And we know that.

Eventually we want to have a family…that'll be a challenge for sure.

But I decided to spend my life with Elizabeth because she makes me feel great…even when I suck.

I just don't ever want to be without him. So…don't go anywhere, okay?

Okay.

ODE TO JOY

Hilary, 40

JM, 33

married 7 years

JM and Hilary show up on my doorstep with a bag of oranges. "We didn't know what to bring, but we didn't want to show up empty handed," Hilary explains. JM is wearing white and black striped tights, has a barrette in her hair and is very quiet. "Do you guys want something to drink?" I ask. "I'll just have water, thanks," JM whispers. "Just so you know, you don't have to talk about anything you don't want to talk about." I say to JM. "Oh no, I'm good," she says, "I think I just accidentally came out to the rest of my family on Facebook today when I changed my profile picture, so bring it on!"

I'm Hilary and I'm forty.

I'm JM and I'm thirty-three.

We've been married for seven years and have been together for nine. But we've known each other for ten.

We met at the theatre. A friend of mine asked me to help out because they were short a few people backstage. That night Hilary almost fired me because I broke the set.

She let go of the wrong drop and it broke the set onstage. Then, when she pulled the drop back up, chunks of wood fell on the actors. I told her, one, not to touch <u>anything</u> anymore and, two, if I had anyone to replace her, I would fire her right now. But I didn't, so I was stuck with her and she'd better not do anything like that again…then a year later we started dating.

By some miracle I was allowed to come back and help out with other shows. One evening, after Hilary and I had worked together for about a year, we were having a conversation with someone we were working with…

Quick question…are we going to get into the fact that all of this happened while JM was a <u>man</u>?

Oh, that's right. There you go.

Part of the reason I asked her back to do some other shows was because she (at the time, he) was really strong and I needed people who could do heavy lifting backstage.

So we started dating when I was a man.

She hadn't come out yet. Hadn't even come out to herself yet, really.

Well I had some idea. Not a whole lot made sense though.

So we had a conversation after a show one evening, and began talking about relationships. I said that I believed the man should always ask the woman out, which is amusing now that I'm in a lesbian relationship. But I said that I usually had to ask the man out and I didn't like it. I wanted to have an old fashioned relationship where I got asked out first.

And I said, "Well what if the person wants to ask you out but has been shot down a lot and is afraid?"

And I said, "Well then the person should just have the courage to ask me out especially if they can be assured that I'll say yes." This went on for about <u>four</u> hours.

I didn't get it…but then the next day we talked for a little while more…and I got the message then.

She said, "Would it be alright if I kissed you? Because if I don't, I think I'm gonna die." I said, "Yes." And we've been together ever since!

So then we had our first date. We went to Santa Monica and ate at this little pie shop called "Polly's House of Pies." And then we walked on the pier.

JM had made a mixed tape for our first date and one of the songs on the tape was "Ode to Joy."

The electronic version from "Clockwork Orange."

So we drove home in my red convertible on this beautiful July evening and blasted that song. That was actually the song we played during our first dance at our wedding, which confounded our families.

On that same ride home, I asked Hilary to pull over and I told her I needed to tell her something. I said, "I don't really understand what this is or how to say it, but I really like you a lot and I'd like to keep going out with you. I don't want you to find this out about me after we've been dating for a while. I think you should find out now."

It was literally that long, this preface to this big, huge statement, so I'm thinking, "Okay, he's married. He's got kids..." I mean what could it be? And then he blurted out, "Sometimes, I wear women's clothing."

Is that what I said? I was so nervous, I don't even remember.

And I looked at him and said, "Okay..." I was still kind of waiting for the big thing. And I said, "Is that it?"

"Well...yeah."

I said, "Well, I don't care."

That was amazing. It was the first time I ever told anyone about this part of me, and Hilary completely accepted it.

But it became very clear as we talked through things that it wasn't just a matter of putting on women's clothing sometimes. JM felt more comfortable as a woman than as a man.

Or rather, I just felt comfortable!

There were things that she identified within herself that were much more female than male. So it was a process. It went from, "I sometimes like wearing women's clothing" to, "I like wearing women's clothing because it makes me feel comfortable" to, "I feel more comfortable as a woman than as a man" to, "I should be a woman."

And even though I didn't understand it, I always had some idea. I've described it before like this: When you're a little kid and you learn how to put on your own shoes, some days you walk outside and you're not sure why, but you feel weird. Then someone points out that you've got your shoes on the wrong feet. And it's like, "Oh! Well, let me just fix that!" Being this way, you don't know that your shoes are on the wrong feet. You just walk around feeling like something's off. Until suddenly you get it. And you feel better.

We dated for about a year and a half before we got engaged.

I didn't have the patience to get on my knee and all of that. I wish I had figured out a way to be nice about it, but I just wanted it to happen so badly.

We were laying next to each other on the futon mattress on the floor of our new apartment. There was nothing else in the room, so it echoed every time you spoke, and JM said to me, "This is good. You wanna do it forever?" It was pouring down rain. I said, "Um...sure?" Then I poked her and said, "Um, what do you mean?"

"Do you want to get married?"

And I did the girl thing. "Oh my god, yes! Did you get a ring?"

"Can we afford a ring?"

"Yes. Of <u>course</u> we can afford a ring." Then two or three days later we went to Target, because we knew what budget we had, and I picked out the five rings that I liked.

Then I picked out the ring I liked from those five and proposed.

In the Target parking lot.

In the rain.

The problem with getting married was I wasn't Catholic and I wasn't going to convert, so JM's family wasn't going to help us out. And my dad had already paid for my pretty princess wedding, so I wasn't getting another one. I was twenty-two when I got married before. I was far too young and it lasted for only three years.

I watched a lot of TV when I was kid. That was basically how I learned how to speak English. I saw a special when I was thirteen about people who got married in Vegas by Elvis impersonators, and it was the most amazing thing I'd ever seen! It was so crazy. I totally wanted that to happen to me.

So we began to look at different venues for the wedding and realistically I realized we couldn't afford anything else. I was like, "JM, if you want the Elvis wedding, lets do it." So we went online and found the place that had the most Elvis choices…

And was the least, you know, ridiculous looking…

I remember calling the place in January to make a reservation for July and the woman said, "You realize it's January…are you sure you mean July? We've never booked someone that far in advance." So July 16th, 2005 we got married by Elvis! He was actually a really good Elvis impersonator. He sang four songs.

We got married by black leather Elvis. '68 comeback special Elvis. Not fat, white, jumpsuit Elvis.

There are a number of Elvis choices.

I think there's actually a Mexican Elvis isn't there? El*vis.*

In all of our pictures, you can see signs in the background that say "Nude!" It's really classy. Then we went to the "Ice Bar" and had our reception. His family stayed on one side of the room and my family stayed on the other.

Like a seventh grade dance.

They didn't talk to each other at all. His family all spoke Spanish and my entire family spoke English. But then we went to his cousin's house and had a grill party.

Yes, the big carne asada party.

It was so much fun. Everyone had a few shots of tequila and then no one really cared that they didn't speak the same language.

After we got married we lived in a teeny tiny studio apartment in Glendale for about five years.

No. Not about five years. It was five years. That was fun. "I'm mad at you so I'm going to go to…the bathroom!" The bathroom was the only place you could go and slam the door.

We somehow didn't kill each other. But I found out during that time that I'm really fussy about things. I really do like things to be in a particular order.

And most of the time I'm pretty laid back about stuff. To be completely fair, in our relationship I am the guy.

We have a lot of basic ways in which we deal with life that are not the same.

For example, I'm very much someone who says, "Okay, we're upset. So we're going to sit here and talk about why we're upset until we're not upset anymore."

For me it's, "I'm upset now. It needs to wear off. I need to be alone."

The way in which we try to resolve issues with one another is not compatible. But we try to focus on the fact that we both are trying to resolve the issues, rather than just focusing on the issue itself.

Sometimes we don't know how to fix things in the same way, but we do know we want the same thing fixed.

It always comes down to, "Do I dislike this thing we're fighting about more than I like JM?" I really have to focus on the things I love about her and not the things that annoy me.

Basically we accept each other for who we are and just focus on all the good in our relationship. As weird and uncomfortable as things sometimes get, the good stuff is so much bigger and better than the bad stuff could ever be. We focus on the good stuff so the bad stuff never becomes big. We move on.

The funny thing is, she just came out to most of our friends and family last October, and the biggest response I got was, "Are you okay with this?" I mean, of course I am! I've known all along. And I've identified as bisexual for most of my adult sexual life, so it's not a big deal at all. I just love JM. The person she is. And for the most part all of our family and friends have been very supportive.

It is confusing for a lot of people. I am transgender. Transgender basically means that your outside parts don't match your inside parts. And whatever stage you're in, whether it's taking surgical measures or hormone therapy or just wearing the right kind of stuff, all of that falls under transgender. And that is a really big umbrella.

But the basis of it is that the psychological person and emotional person do not match the physiological person. Then there are cross dressers, who have no desire to be the other gender; they just like wearing clothing of the other gender. Eddie Izzard is an example. He flat out says that he likes to wear women's clothing. He doesn't want to be a woman. Then transsexual is a term that is usually used right before or right after surgery.

But I don't think being surgically altered is the way I want to go personally. You may not like the shape of your foot, but it's still your foot!

It has been interesting though, being in a relationship where JM has been going openly from a man to a woman. Evidently the most common way of dealing with "the change" is cutting off everyone who knew you as a man. It makes sense. That way, when you move to a new city, you move in as that new gender, so no one ever questions it. JM didn't do that, which I'm grateful for, but it makes it much harder for her. I'll have people who I don't even really know ask me, "Is he going to get his parts cut off?" And it's like, why would that be any of your business? I don't walk up to you and ask about your sex life.

Just in general, don't ask about anyone's genitals. It's weird. And it's rude.

But now that she identifies as a female, it has become open rein. Everyone feels like they can ask about our sex life. And the weird thing is, they don't ask her…they ask me. To some extent, it'd be less weird if they asked her. I mean, if you want to be that personal with a transgender, ask the transgender person. It's an odd opening up of what people find appropriate to ask all of a sudden.

You can ask me where I got my shoes, where I got my nails done, who does my eyebrows. All that's fine. Pretty much anything outside of my underwear is fine.

You can even ask me about my underwear! Just, come on. Don't go there.

I didn't know that you could be a transgender male to female <u>and</u> be a lesbian. I didn't get that. For a long time I thought to myself, "Well, I've got male parts and I like lady clothes, does this mean that I like guys too?" And at one point I tried to test it. And after it was over, I thought to myself, "Well how did that go?" And it went okay. It was a little stubbly, which was weird, but I kind of enjoyed it because the whole time I was thinking about beautiful women that I would like to be kissing. Oh, wait! I guess I don't like guys if I have to think about women while I'm making out with a good-looking man.

There's usually no switch when transgender people come out. Guys that I've known who were straight and went from a man to a woman usually became lesbians. Guys who were gay and went from a man to a woman, then became hetero. Who you are attracted to is certainly more identified with the inside you than the physiological you. From what I've seen though, it's much easier to be a gay man and go to being a heterosexual woman than it is going from being a lesbian to a heterosexual man. I guess in a way, a heterosexual man wouldn't like a lesbian and a lesbian wouldn't want to be with a heterosexual man. It seems much more difficult for women to "let it go." I suppose that's the way women are with everything, right? I mean, no offense, but men are usually like, "Sex! Okay!" And as long as you have the parts they're attracted to, that's fine.

In many ways, the transition has been easier for me than JM. I mean, there were some adjustments that I needed to make. I married a man who I was very much in love with and the person is still there, but the guy is not there anymore. It's a matter of thinking to myself, "Okay, I am no longer in a heterosexual relationship, I am now in a lesbian relationship." And at least I have been in one before so it wasn't like I had to suddenly decide if I wanted to be a lesbian. We've had the joke for a long time that if JM was going to fall in love with someone, it's a good thing it was me because I'm the only one who would stick with her. My role has very much been sitting back, observing, and being there to support when I need to. It has almost been a passive journey for me. There are things that I have been aware of before JM was willing to admit them. I've had to sit back and not help, because she needs to make these realizations on her own. And I've realized that I'm really bad at not telling people what to do and when to do it.

I have expected almost everything JM has said to me since the change. I've just been waiting for her to realize it. A few weeks after she came out she said to me, "Honey, I'm a lesbian." And I said, "Well good, 'cause if you dumped me now, I'd be pissed!"

It's just a matter of making all the pieces fit in your head. You're putting together the puzzle without knowing what the box looks like.

I have no way of knowing how hard it's been for her because all I've had to do is sit there and watch. I just have my arms wide open if she needs me. But we've been really lucky. Her work has been supportive, my family has been supportive, and it seems like her family is okay with it.

I wrote a letter to my mom last year. We went over to her house, she read it and then she started sobbing. When she finally stopped, she looked at Hilary and said, "This means you're not going to love him anymore."

And I was like, "No! I've known for a long time! We're good!" So we're not sure if she accepts JM, but she has said that she loves me more than she's ever loved me before. So I'm good.

Yeah, she likes Hilary now.

We've had a tough road, his mom and I. She didn't like me at first because I was divorced. I am also seven years older than JM. And I'm only ten years younger than her, which becomes creepy because she physically can't be my mom.

And you're white.

There's that. So I've had a bumpy road with the family. But evidently me staying with their son when he became their daughter is the thing that has made it all okay. I'm in! Although after we told his mom that "he" was now a "she" we were given two pictures of Jesus to put up in our apartment…

One of them is Mormon Jesus. And he's actually a really good lookin' fella. But the other Jesus is Mexican Jesus, who was the Jesus in the town where she grew up.

And he's scary! He's the Jesus that you don't piss off.

He's the recently crucified, bloody, just, "up to here with it" Jesus. "Oh really? You woke me up for this? This better be good."

It's intense.

The parties, celebrations and rituals that go along

with Mexican Catholicism are a lot of fun. The icons and stuff? They are scary as hell.

Which is the point I guess: Scary. As. Hell.

My mom's not happy with me coming out. I know that. But I'm still her son and as long as I'm happy and I'm not hurting anyone, it's probably okay.

A friend of JM's said something to me at my bachelorette party that I don't think was meant to be very nice, but it ended up being a very correct statement. She had known JM since high school and she said, "I'm glad you guys got together because we didn't think anyone would be able to deal with him." It was a slam on him and kind of a slam on me. It was just such an odd statement. But the fact is, it's true. We're pretty much the only people that can get along with each other. We don't ever need a break.

For the most part, I don't like most people. I mean, come on, have you met most people? But Hilary is the only person that I'm okay being around all the time.

She's my best friend. I hear people say, "Oh I can't talk about that with my boyfriend," or wife or whatever. And the fact is, nothing is off limits with us. You should never have to hold anything back with someone you're with.

I've known people who say, "Well, we really don't have anything in common." You don't need to. I mean, don't get me wrong. Your basic values have to be the same. If Hilary suddenly said, "Hey, there's this KKK rally I'm going to go check out," well, then we'd have a problem. But there just has to be a willingness to say, "Okay, you care about this. I'm going to find out why you care about this."

Because of our willingness to try stuff out for one another, we end up in some really interesting situations. For example, on our anniversary we took a ride in an open cockpit in a biplane. It never would have occurred to me to buy that for myself, but I wanted to get it for her. Then I found out that they did aerobatics! We were doing flips and all sorts of things!

I had cloud in my mouth!

It was fantastic! And it's not something I would've ever thought of doing for myself. I ended up adoring it. You don't have to care about the same things; you just have to care about the fact that your partner cares about those things. And you have to be willing to understand <u>why</u> your partner cares about those things. Another example, I love to listen to NPR all the time. JM would rather shoot herself in the foot. But she's now heard some stuff that she's interested in.

It turns out that I'm interested in politics. Who knew?

We've broadened each other's horizons, big time. We don't have to have everything in common because that would be really boring. But the fact is, there are things I would never have even known about if I hadn't met her.

I knew right away that I wanted to spend my life with Hilary. I said to myself, "Oh, this is what people talk about! I want to spend the rest of my life with this person! Forever!"

It sort of became, how can we <u>not</u> spend the rest of our lives together? If I wasn't with her, I'd spend all my time wanting to tell her stuff. If I wasn't with her, then I'd never hear her laugh like Ricky Ricardo ever again. When she laughs really hard, she sounds exactly like Ricky Ricardo from "I Love Lucy." And she has the *most screwball sense of humor. She will say things to me that make absolutely no sense and then she will laugh her head off. It is the most joyful thing I've ever seen. I adore that about her. I have no idea what makes her laugh, but I'll just sit there and eventually I'll start laughing too. The idea of not having her in my life is unacceptable to me. I obviously understand that one of us will die someday. We've actually talked about this. We want to be really old and we want to go out together. Because at this point it's not, "Well I guess I'm gonna stay with her for the rest of my life," it's, "I can't <u>not</u> be with her.*

It's kind of corny, but we really did get made for each other.

In an odd, odd way. We're so corny together but it works.

Did you say horny or corny?

Corny!

But the other one too.

A WHIRLWIND ROMANCE

Gail, 50

Ted, 58

married 11 years

I get a text from Gail: "We're running late! We were at the bar! Needed to get properly loosened up for the interview!" As I wait outside their house, I take a good look. The entire structure is made out of metal. When they first built it over ten years ago, I remember how confused I was. It was like some strange space station from the future…and it was pretty ugly. I had always wanted to see the inside though, and would soon get my chance. Gail and Ted pull into the driveway. "Sorry, sorry!" She says, "We had a few beers. But this is going to be a good interview!" Ted is confused. "What are you interviewing us about anyway?" "Oh, Ted it'll be fun. You just have to talk about how much you love me!" Ted is hesitant as we go inside. The inside of the house is absolutely stunning. The living room, dining room and kitchen are all one, big, open space. The floors are concrete and the furniture is made out of recycled materials. "Wow," I say, "This house is amazing! I've never seen anything like this before!" "Yup!" Gail says, "And entirely eco-friendly! Hey, I think I may need just one more beer while we're talking…is that okay?"

Hi, my name is Gail. I've been married to Ted for eleven years now and I just had my fiftieth birthday.

I'm Ted.

My lovely husband.

I'm fifty-eight and a half and I have been married the same number of years. We met through a personal ad in the newspaper.

I placed the ad.

Gail placed the ad.

I had gone through the horrible process of moving here from San Francisco. I had taken a job at a small company and it was really tough being in a brand new town. Then a good friend of mine from San Francisco came to visit and said, "Come on! It's not that bad, you just have to get out there and meet some guys." So she wrote an ad for me in the paper and Ted wrote me back.

This was pre-email, so personal ads were still going strong. I had been divorced for about eight years and had been going through the dating scene. I was going through a lot of difficult situations, but I decided to give it one last try. I went through four month's worth of papers and handpicked women who sounded like they might be interesting to meet. I thought all the good ones would be taken, but it was worth a shot.

Meanwhile, I was spending $1.99 a minute to listen to these duds who would call me and leave horrible messages. Guys who would ramble, run out of time, call back and ramble some more about <u>nothing</u>. It was awful. I never called any of them back. Then I got the phone bill. That was shocking. But then I started to get *letters, and the letters were much more interesting. When I got Ted's letter it was so nice! There was a little picture of him, stamp sized, in the corner. And he was really into recycling and Eco Living, so it was cool to see someone who was passionate about something that I was passionate about. Anyway, I got his letter and I slept with it under my pillow. I guess I was either desperate or excited.*

You were desperate? You never told me that.

Okay, well I just had this feeling about it. I would call his number that was at the bottom of the letter, but I kept getting his answering machine. Finally he answered and we had a nice conversation over the phone.

We met for the first time at a restaurant for lunch. I walked in and Gail was sitting at the bar. I didn't know what she looked like so I got a table, sat down and then Gail came over and introduced herself.

Yes and the big thing that Ted didn't do when I got to the table was he didn't stand up.

She thought that was rude.

I did, but we ended up having a very nice lunch.

I had just come back from a workshop at the Esalen institute in California. I forget what the name of the workshop was, but one of the issues was talking about your parents. One of the things that came up for me was that I had never told my dad that I loved him. So that was very emotional for me. I remember talking with Gail about that and I actually got sort of teary eyed.

Teared up. At lunch. First date.

It was a little embarrassing. Not the sort of thing you're supposed to do when you first meet someone.

But it was nice in a way. I mean it was a little awkward, but deep. I mean, every time I see my parents I tell them I love them, so I was interested. He was different from my family. I liked that.

I didn't turn her off that much I guess. So we had a couple of dates, and then Gail went to Israel for three weeks. When she got back, everything sped up. It was a whirlwind romance. Let's see, we had our first date in February, she went to Israel, came back, we went to Paris in July and got engaged there. Now that I think about it, it was a tad fast.

Ted had a family member getting married in France and it was a big "to do" wedding. Fireworks, a chateau, big boat rides out in the ocean. It was spectacular. We had a wonderful time and he proposed. I said yes.

She didn't even hesitate.

Well it was very romantic! I had such a good feeling when I first met Ted. It was emotional right away. It was gripping. I realized right away that I had to ask myself if I was ready to commit. And I was. It was just great being with him. And then, right after we got engaged, I realized I was pregnant.

So we were married in November and had our son Gabriel in May of 2001.

Both of us had been married before. I was married for six years. After that ended, it was ten years before I met Ted.

And I had been divorced for about eight or nine years when we met.

I learned a lot in my first marriage about what I wanted and didn't want when I did get married again. I think Ted and I were just at a point where we were both willing to commit.

As far as settling down goes.

I had done my career out in California. That wasn't important to me anymore. I really wanted to raise a family and settle down. So then we came home, had Gabriel, and started building our house. And, as I said before, Ted and I are both into recycling.

Well, that's kind of an understatement.

Our house is <u>entirely</u> eco-friendly. Our only requirement for the building site was sunlight, and lots of it. Ted used to manufacture solar energy systems so he wanted to combine his solar and recycling know-how to build a house that utilized both recyclable and recycled materials.

It was Earth friendly, but very unconventional.

Yes. Unconventional is the word. When we finished building and started to move in, we got an anonymous note that read, "We can't believe you built this ugly house here. It's going to drive down all our home values." Right after we moved in, two neighbors installed eight-foot fences and another built a pagoda to block the view. Ted is the town's recycling coordinator and he wasn't worried about the negative reaction. He kind of took it as a sign that we were doing the right thing. Soon after we moved in, we invited everyone in the neighborhood over for an open house to clear the air.

It took some people a while to get used to it, but once we talked about it everyone understood the green aspects and wanted to learn more.

Anyway, building our house was a big deal. I was pretty much a single parent for fourteen months.

When you build a house, and a life, a lot of things don't go the way you want them to. You have to make a lot of adjustments. It's the art of learning to adjust. You accept what works and discover what's realistic, and you learn to be happy with what works between you. I think the fact that we got together as two fairly older people...

Ahem. I was only thirty-seven!

Well, we were set in our ways. And that makes it a little harder to make adjustments than if we were younger.

But we're making them. It's interesting how we go through all these cycles together. How we rub off on each other and how we become more like each other. I'm not quite as thin as Ted yet, but I'm working on it.

Our love has definitely gotten stronger.

It sort of changes over the years. You learn more about each other; you learn your rhythms.

It's pretty amazing living together, being together and just getting a new appreciation of each other. And we've gone through a lot of difficulties. With building this house, and raising Gabriel...

The death of my father. Ted's mother moving in here.

All of those things you go through. And you grow stronger just by learning how to deal with all of those issues together. It's an interesting process. We've made it through the seven-year-itch, so that's a good thing.

Seven-year-itch?

Yeah, I think a lot of relationships end after seven years. It's sort of a point where you either make it or you don't. We're on eleven years now, so I think we're good.

I hope so!

But being together, staying together and putting up with one another...there's a lot of growth that comes with that. It's a process. When I met Gail I had a gut feeling. You read about those speed-dating things where you meet a lot of people in a short amount of time...well, part of me thinks that is a valid concept. When you meet someone, in that first minute or two, a lot of times you get a fairly accurate impression of whether or not there's some compatibility there. And I just knew when I met Gail. It's hard to put into words what exactly it was, but I felt it.

He knew I was a keeper.

Yeah, I guess I did.

THE THING TO DO

Andrea, 31

Jacob, 37

together 8 years

Andrea and Jacob have been together eight years and despite external pressures from family and society, have decided not to marry…yet.

My name is Andrea and I am thirty-one years old.

My name is Jacob and I'm thirty-seven years old. I guess we met nine or ten years ago.

I think it was longer than that…I was twenty or twenty-one so it was ten years ago and we've been dating for eight years…

So the story is that we happened to move into the same apartment while I was in graduate school at the University of Chicago and Andrea was finishing up her undergrad.

Jacob was already living in the apartment and I was getting out of a bad roommate situation. I thought it would just be till the end of that school year but I ended up staying in that apartment till I graduated, so actually another year and a half.

It was one of those apartments that had people living there who didn't spend much time in the apartment together…so I guess it was really six or seven months after she moved in that we became friend-ly.

When you're in undergrad you think that grad students are sort of…old…you know? It's just a different type of life. But we were brought together as "friends" because we were the only clean people in the apartment. We lived with a forty-seven-year-old man who was basically a hoarder. We each had our own room, but the rest of the apartment was his place so we didn't spend too much time in the common areas.

Andrea was a brave young woman moving in with four male graduate students. She was obviously very desperate or daring, or both. She seemed very quiet, maybe a little timid…

I remember a couple of months after I moved in, my parents and siblings were in town. And I wanted to show them my apartment. I didn't want to go there that much because it wasn't really a place where you could hang out. So we stopped there briefly. During the visit I had to go get the car with my dad and I was like, "Jacob can you just stay with my family while I run out? I'll be right back."

When I came back, Jacob was getting out popsicles for everyone. He was more hospitable than I could ever hope to be. So I was like, wow, this guy is all right. Of course it's colored now by the fact that we are together so I can look back on it as part of our relationship almost. But it wasn't even in the context of that. This was years before we started dating.

The shift started happening when I was living in Ann Arbor, about a year after I graduated. Jacob's sister was in for cancer treatments at the hospital and I just wanted to stop by, say hi, and see if there was anything to be done.

I was really grateful to see a familiar, friendly face. We sat in the hospital together that whole night. My sister was getting an extended MRI and so Andrea and I were catching up in this weird basement hallway with no windows. This was an incredibly emotional time for me…

My sister, who was an amazing individual, actually had spinal taps without anesthesia. She disliked the nausea brought on by the anesthesia more than she disliked the pain of the actual spinal tap. So she was wracked with these pain spasms. Now there were certain parts of her body that you could press to somehow distract or alleviate the pain. So we're sitting there, I hadn't seen Andrea in a year, and we're squeezing and grabbing my sister while she's screaming. It was really intense.

Afterwards, we took my sister back to her hotel and I was going to drive Andrea home…

And as we were walking through the parking lot, I grabbed Jacob's hand. I don't usually do that sort of thing, but it felt like the right thing to do.

And then I kissed her…it was a really intense evening…

So, I was still living in Ann Arbor and Jacob was in Chicago. It's actually ironic that we got together at this time because we were no longer at the same place, after pretty much living together for years. So I would go to Chicago when I wasn't working and he would come here to see his family and his sister. We did that for two years.

Eight months after we first started dating, my sister was in the final stages of her cancer and Andrea was coming from Ann Arbor to central Michigan, where my parents lived, to help out with the family. The first year of our relationship was not what you'd call ideal circumstances by any stretch of the imagination. Well, the external circumstances anyway.

In 2006, I moved back to Chicago and started doing research for my former college advisor. We lived in an apartment together briefly and then I moved into a co-op closer to campus. I lived there a full year before Jacob moved in. So we definitely took our time...

We're <u>still</u> taking our time. As far as marriage goes…

I never thought I would get married when I was young. I never had those sorts of fantasies. I guess I could see myself getting married now. I mean, just with Jacob. Not like I'm gonna go to Vegas or something and just do it. But to me the ceremony is not the important part. What's important is making a commitment to somebody. It doesn't have to be in a public setting and verified by the church and the law. One of the things that has changed my mind about getting married is that it is so difficult to make that commitment in an alternative way and still have the same rights. But the ceremony doesn't really matter. It's not important to me. But it's different for Jacob...

I put a fair bit of value on getting married. Obviously I don't put sufficient value on it for it to have happened already, but it's something that is really important to me and I suspect that it is something that will happen. We had a very long rough patch for about three years. Some of it was emotional fallout from my sister's cancer and death. That really wore us out and we were just trying to hold ourselves together. So back then getting married would've been a really bad idea.

In a way, it's considered the "thing to do" when you get to a certain age, especially in our tradition. So at a time when we were both really suffering from depression, we were getting questions like, "So, when are you getting married?" It was really annoying. I just wanted to say, "Really people, this is not at the top of the priority list at the moment!"

And there was never a point where things magically got better either. There was never a Thursday morning where we suddenly got up and said, "Yay! We're so much better now! Now we can get married!" There was a long, gradual "getting better" process. Marriage is something that we can, and have talked about, but for a long time it wasn't an option. It has come to a point now where we've had to ask ourselves if we individually feel strong enough to make that kind of commitment to each other.

It's never easy. Or, if it was easy, I would question it. But I think about how different we are. And how different I am from when we started dating. It took a lot to change certain aspects of myself but I believed it was good to at least try and see if I could be slightly different. It's not like night and day or anything. But, for example, I don't really talk that much and somehow there's this expectation that when you're with someone you share all your thoughts together. Well, that's something I don't easily do. I especially don't talk through my decisions. I just focus on the end point. But collective decision-making is something that is important to do in a relationship, so I have consciously tried to do that. I think that's really valuable, and I never would've had the drive to do it by myself.

I am definitely a different person in this relationship than I was when we first started out. But a lot of that is because of outside factors. Both my sister and my mom went through extended periods and struggles with cancer, which they ultimately didn't defeat. So that has colored my outlook in a lot of respects. I think I'm a sadder person than I was when we first started dating. And that's not a bad thing. It's just a thing.

But some of what Andrea alludes to regarding collective decision-making and talking things through…I am very much the sort of person who does that. In fact I can recall being a little boy and noticing how stereotypically in adult couples, the guy was the one who was non-communicative or had trouble verbalizing his emotions and the woman was looking for a certain kind of companionship. So at a very young age I decided, "Hey look, I can do that. That I can do!"

But then he fell in love with me. So that goes to show you, you can't plan anything.

It has taken a lot for me to realize that most of the time when Andrea is quiet, it doesn't necessarily mean that she's:

A. Mad.

B. Suppressing something. Or,

C. Resentful of something that I've done.

But a particular kind of silence is sometimes just that. If anything it's just her sign for, "Give me a little bit of space." I mean, I can be around people all day. I am a very social person. And Andrea isn't. She isn't anti-social, but she is asocial in some respects.

When we first started to butt heads in this relationship it took us a while to realize that although there are a lot of intellectual commonalities and attitudinal commonalities between the two of us, there are deeper, underlying differences between us as well.

I think from my family experience, I like to hash things out. A lot of self-help books talk about how you and your significant other should never go to bed angry. You should always talk things out so you can wake up the next morning and have everything be clear. Well, that does not work in our relationship.

Yeah, I'm pretty much like, "No! Just let me go to bed! Please!!!"

Yeah, "I want to suppress this and go to bed, thanks. Put it on a shelf and forget about it." So if we had gotten married when I wanted to, we would've encountered this problem in the first year and a half of our marriage. And I don't know. I mean, I would like to think that we wouldn't have gotten divorced over that, but who knows? It would've been really tough.

For me, living together has actually made a lot of things easier. Moving in together, even in the context of living with thirteen other people in this co-op, has made it almost harder to escape. You just work things out. That was a turning point in our relationship. A confirmation of, okay, we can do this.

I actually asked one of our roommates who lives next door to us if he ever hears anything from our room. We like to think that we're pretty quiet about our problems. We don't throw cutlery or anything.

And he said, "Well, sometimes I hear Jacob's voice saying something, and then I just hear this hysterical laughter." And I was like, "Yeah, that's pretty accurate."

I think a lot of the reason why we've worked as a couple is because our humor is so similar. We make each other laugh.

I often think about people who get married young and develop collectively. Because when you get married at twenty something you haven't really developed as yourself before you've gotten involved in this binding relationship. And that's neither bad nor good...but I think getting married young changes how you develop. I think you develop a certain way based on the kind of relationship you are in. And I do feel that because Jacob and I didn't get married right away, we were able to develop into two whole individuals.

Everyone has a honeymoon period. But in a way we sort of had the bad fortune to have the good luck to not get married right away. I was ready to get married probably a year or so after we started dating and then all these horrible outside circumstances happened. After that I began to notice patterns between us. Like, "Oh, Andrea behaves <u>this</u> way and I behave <u>that</u> way...hmmm, I thought it was just stylistic or whatever, but these differences run deep!"

But despite these differences, we know that we're in it for the long run. We love each other and we are completely committed to each other. I mean, I knew I loved Jacob before we even got together. That first night in the parking lot I said it.

I think it took me about nine months to figure out that I loved Andrea. I knew I liked her and I admired her. That's a funny word. That you <u>admire</u> someone. It's not the first thing you think of. "Lust after," yes. "Think is beautiful," yes. "Have a great time with," yes. But admire? That's kind of a weird thing to say.

Well, we're kind of weird. So it works!

FIGURE IT OUT

Joelle, 67

married 13 years to Aaron, deceased.

I've lived down the street from Joelle for about twenty-five years. I grew up and went to school with her two daughters, Abby and Leah. Although I knew she had lost her husband, I never asked her about him or questioned why her two girls grew up without a father.

My name is Joelle and I'm sixty-seven. My husband's name was Aaron. I met him in 1970 through what they called "computer dating." But it wasn't really computer dating the way it is these days. It was just a computer that matched people up.

I knew I wanted somebody who was Jewish, older than I was, and educated. But during that time, there were these co-eds being killed. Girls were being murdered all over town. They all were 5'5" and had brown hair and brown eyes. I had a professor in child psychology when I was in grad school who actually called three of us up to his desk and said, "Here's my card." We all just stared blankly at him and he said, "Well look at you, what do all three of you have in common?" And we were all 5'5" with brown eyes and brown hair. He said, "If anyone comes up to you and you're not sure what to do, just stick your knee between his legs and here's my card for when the police pick you up. I will come down and bail you out." That's how serious it was.

So I had to stop dating for a while because it wasn't safe. They finally caught the man who was doing it, but they could only prove that he murdered one of the girls. It turns out that I had actually danced with him once at a singles club.

Anyway, I was trying to get back in the field again and so I signed up for "computer dating." And that's how I met my husband. I was about twenty-four.

On our first date we went to the movies. I believe it was "Butch Cassidy and the Sundance Kid." And on our second date we went drag racing down Telegraph Road. He was a grad student in bioelectric engineering, which was kind of a new field back then, and I was teaching.

I was dating other people too, but we were in our mid-twenties, and by then you know what you want. I hated dating. I really hated dating all those different people. And when I started dating Aaron, within six months I knew I wanted to get married. We got married in June of '71 so we must've gotten engaged less than a year after we met.

He had no choice but to propose. I was about to move to California. I didn't really _want_ to go, but it was a threat to get him to ask me to marry him. I don't remember the proposal though. Was it romantic? I guess not if I can't remember it. Did he get down on his knee? No, because I helped design the ring. In other words it was, get off your rear end and do something…or I'm leaving. It worked.

He was a diabetic. Had juvenile diabetes. He was very active, but the leading cause of blindness in the world is called diabetic retinopathy. What happens is, extra blood vessels grow on your eye. Nowadays they zap and kill them with lasers. Well, of course there were no lasers back then.

So we got married and then a few years later his eyesight started to go. That's when we made the decision that until things were stable we were not going to have kids. We were married for nine years before we had kids. He was totally blind. We had all sorts of drama from '75-'78. He went completely blind the summer of '78, and he spent that summer with his parents. Then he came back here and started his corporation in our basement. His corporation made one of the first talking computers in the United States. There were twenty-five talking computers around the country at that time, and his was one of them.

First he made what was called the "Cyber-Typer," for blind people. You'd press the key and it told you what key it was. I think that went down to some various rehab centers. That invention eventually evolved into a talking computer, but you needed a lot of money to make something like that happen and when IBM went *into it, we just couldn't compete.*

My oldest daughter was born in September of 1980. We decided he was blind, and was not going to see anymore, but that shouldn't stop us from living the life we wanted to live. He still went through Lamaze classes with me and the doctor's decided since he wasn't going to see the birth, they would put a student nurse in there with us. Her job was to describe the birthing to him tell him what was going on: "Now the head's coming out, it's all slimy, whatever, blah, blah, blah." The problem was, she had never seen a birth before. So she started to scream and yell, and Aaron kept saying, "What's wrong? What's happening?" He thought there was something seriously wrong with the baby, you know? So finally the doctor had to kick that girl out. Then they moved him up near me and when our daughter was born, they put her in a towel and plopped her on his lap. Said, "Okay, you figure it out."

He took care of our daughter, Abby, for her first year of life. I had her and went back to work after six to eight weeks. Every morning I would change her diaper and put bells on her rear end. There was a playpen in the basement (the basement was his office) and he would change her diaper every few hours. He'd treat every diaper like it was loaded. We had a system: he'd change the diaper, put it in a plastic bag, wipe her rear end and that was that. So he completely took care of her.

We'd have a babysitter come in the afternoon usually and every Friday night she would stay and we'd go out. He was stuck in the house you know.

Abby was five and a half and Leah was two when he passed away. He had a kidney transplant that didn't take and a blood clot that went to his heart.

I happened to be home that day. May of 1986. Our nanny

couldn't come because she was sick so I just happened to be around. Fate was that way. He said, "I don't feel well." We called the physical therapist and she came as she was told to and exercised him. But what happened was there was a blood clot in his leg and the movement of the physical therapy made it go to his heart. And that's how he died. He had been sitting around because it had been about two or three weeks since the transplant.

It was horrible then, but everybody knew he was sick. He was much sicker than I thought he was. Than I could realize, I guess. He'd been in and out of the hospital for about a year and a half. And when I look back on it, he had no quality of life left because the kidney transplant hadn't taken.

But it is interesting because before we had our second baby girl, he had a complete physical. In September of '83, the doctors told him he was as healthy as could be. Blind, but healthy. "Go ahead and have another kid!" They told us. Leah was born in June of '84, and about a year and a half later he died. That is how fast diabetes goes. And that is what diabetes does.

I thought about getting married again after he passed away. For the companionship, you know. But I was so busy teaching full time and taking care of the kids that I never really had the time. I did date, but I never brought anybody home.

I never liked dating anyhow. I didn't need the tension of raising kids and the tension of teaching, plus adding a third tension in the form of a guy. So I didn't date much. I never really had the time and I never really felt the need. I was so busy doing what I was doing and when I got time alone I loved it. Whenever I shipped the girls off to overnight camp I would dance around the house.

You're feeling sorry for me. But don't feel sorry for me until the fall of '84. Up until then, we had a pretty normal life. He was *completely self-sufficient. He put the dishes away and made the bed every day. It sounds like hardship, but it wasn't. He was the primary caregiver to Abby. Every night, they played together after dinner. He gave her the bottle and changed her diaper. He did all that stuff. He was there. When she was born, they plopped her into his arms and he sat there counting her fingers over and over.*

We were just a normal couple with kids. We went to the movies and went out to dinner. We had concert seats at the Auditorium downtown. We did everything up until his last year and a half of life. He was just blind.

ANNA BOWEN

THE BEAUTY OF ESTROGEN

Shelly, 49

Adam, 57

married 14 years

*I walk into Shelly and Adam's two bedroom home and am greeted
by Henry, their fat, fluffy, black outdoor cat. Movie posters decorate
the brightly painted walls and a sign that says, "Get Over It" is
above the entrance to the kitchen. As Shelly pours me a glass of
homemade lemonade, Adam nervously stands by the dining room
table in the other room. "Honey, get in here and tell this girl how
much you adore me!" Shelly exclaims, giving me a wink. "Adam's
a little nervous about the interview thing…it's okay, I'll probably
talk the whole time anyway." "You usually do," Adam chuckles,
finally coming out of hiding and into the living room. "Okay," he
sighs, "I'm ready. Let's do this thing."*

How old am I?

Older than me! That's all that matters.

Forty-seven?

You seriously don't know.

No…fifty-seven…

Oh my god. Honey, Alzheimer's is a real thing.

Fifty-seven. And my name's Adam…you're turn…

Oh! Shelly. Forty-nine…dot, dot, dot…and we've been married for…

Twelve years.

Fourteen years. Did you really just say twelve?

Yup.

Oh my god. Well…I actually saw his backside before I saw his front side. He was kneeling on my friend Delaney's porch and looked really cute from behind. He had on shorts and his legs were really tan and his sleeves were rolled up. He was just cute. So I asked Delaney who that cute guy was on her porch and she said, "My <u>handyman</u>?" Then I started to think of a bunch of things that were broken at my house that he could come and fix.

That was the summer of '96.

So that's how we met. I introduced myself to him and Delaney just shook her head.

I remember I came in, I was working on Delaney's dining room ceiling light, and they were sitting at the dining room table getting ready to go downtown to the bars.

Yeah, we did that a lot then. We were hunting for men. "The Brew Pub." That's what happens when two thirty-something women are single.

You were yelling about something.

Yelling?

Yeah. Loud. Like you usually are.

I don't remember that.

I do. So that year, Shelly just kept finding work for me to do at her house.

I thought, for literally over a year, that I was hopelessly flirting. I was <u>really</u> trying. I was dropping off things at his house, like enormous loaves of bread I had baked and invitations to parties. But he never did anything.

Nope. I just didn't go out much.

He was shy.

Well I never had much of a social life after I stopped drinking.

So I was trying to bring a social life to his door. With bread. Ridiculously large loaves of bread.

So finally, Thanksgiving of '97, like a year and a half after we had met, Adam had worked at my house a million times, he said something about going to his sister's house for the holidays. I made a strudel thinking, "Okay, I'll bribe his sister." And that

*worked…kind of. I think she was like, "Who is this woman?"
But Adam gave me this really nice basket of food for Christmas.
Fancy foods. I called my brother and said, "Oh my god, what do I
do with truffles?" And my brother was like, "Okay, here's what
you do, are you having him over for dinner?" And I said, "Yeah,
I'm working on that." So I cooked for him and had him over for
dinner…and he didn't like what I made.*

She made fish. I hate fish.

*Yup. Sorry about that. But that evening, I made my needs
clear! "Soooo, are you going to kiss me?" He was like, "Okay."
Arg! I was banging my head against the wall by that point.*

I just didn't get it.

*That was just after Christmas when we finally kissed and then
he proposed in March. We had only dated for about two and a half
months. But we'd known one another for over a year. Then we were
married in May.*

She was in a real hurry.

I know. I guess I was afraid he was going to get away.

She told the whole neighborhood the next day.

Did I?

Mmhmmm. Went ringing doorbells.

Does that sound like me?

Mmhmmm…and do you remember the engagement
party they threw for us?

Oh yes. So the neighbors threw us an engagement party and

the sangria was really good…and <u>maybe</u> I consumed a little bit too much.

You and Bill got into a pillow fight.

Well there were pillows everywhere and we started whipping them across the room.

And you spilled sangria on Tracy's brand new carpet. The two-day-old carpet.

The white carpet. For some reason, to this day, Tracy still speaks to me.

But you never were invited back.

That's true. I never was. I called the carpet cleaner that night but I'm not sure if they got the stain out. Bill might have not been invited back either…but I bet she doesn't have any more red wine sangria parties! With white carpeting I think white sangria's the way to go…it's delicious.

Anyway, we were in the shower when I proposed.

I couldn't really say no to a naked man. Would've been rude.

But after she said yes, I had to go get the ring.

The ring was his mom's.

She left it to me, and my sister was taking care of it.

And his sister was like, "Who is this woman you're giving it to? Have I ever met her?" And of course, she hadn't. That was rocky at first. When she first met me she would say things like, "Every time I look at that ring on you, I want to take it off. It's supposed to be on my mother's hand." That was weird. But if you think about it, it made sense. You never forget the things your parents wore. I did have another ring that I wore to work though, because I was working in a lot of kitchens and I didn't want to lose this beautiful diamond from his mom. And then I lost that ring, kneading dough or something. Oh man, that would've been bad if I lost his mom's ring. His sister would've hated me.

I had been married before and had two children, Helen and Neal. And Adam is such a kid person that he fit right in with our family. He had been around the house at least a few times a week fixing things and my kids took to him almost instantly. Adam actually talks to kids, you know? He gets down on the floor and talks to them. It was really different and nice to see that. It was huge. But my family was a lot more than just my kids. My family was my former husband and my parents and my neighborhood...so that was a lot.

My family was a lot too.

They were, but they were nice to me.

We figured it all out.

We were really, really lucky. It wasn't a blended family nightmare. My former husband and Adam are very kind to each other. And most importantly, the sharing of the kids has never been an issue. I hear horror stories of divorces and it's just not like that with these guys. I can't even imagine what it could've been like. What some people go through.

But my son, Neal, was unsure of how Adam would work. He was really scared. He thought it was an either-or deal, and if Adam came into our lives, that his own dad would disappear. He was terrified. But his dad was great. He showed up the evening of our wedding and the next day and the day after that just to show Neal that he was still around, and would always be.

My daughter, Helen, was pretty good about it all. She understood that she got love from mom, and from Dad, and now she got even __more__ love from Adam. And she felt really lucky that she got all this love from so many people. But Neal saw it as a loss rather than a gain, and so did Adam's nieces and nephews. Adam was very involved in their lives before I came along, so they wondered how things would change now that he had another family to look after. We thought it was really important to bring the two families together.

And we did that on our honeymoon.

Yup. Our honeymoon was the two of us trapped on a seven-acre island with six children.

One week up north with Shelly's kids and all of my nieces and nephews.

It was __insane__, but we're still here! We actually had a ball. It was the most exhausting week of my entire life. From the get-go it was snakes and frogs and fireworks and tie-dye and making food and trying to get everyone to sleep and god forbid should we have any time alone. It was hysterical.

Six kids all under the age of ten in a small cottage. One bedroom and two rooms with bunk beds.

One bathroom…most of them peed outside. It was crazy.

That could've been a make it or break it situation but it wasn't.

Well we've been through much worse since then. Our love has had a few ebbs.

Has it?

Oh dear god, yes. And it's had some flows. Well that's not true. Not my love, just my "like." We've had some hard times. What couple hasn't?

I haven't.

You haven't now have you?

No. Can't say that I have.

Are you sure?

I'm positive.

I'm going to cry…he's a good liar. It's been crazy.

There have been some events.

Ya think? Yes, there have been a lot of "events." It's funny. This is something I never thought about…but you just think, when you're first together, that love will endure everything and it will be the same. But you forget that <u>you</u> change. And that changes how you relate to each other. I never thought about that. I certainly never thought about that in my first marriage. So it has been really hard. This relationship has been much more "real life." And that's just the way it is. I don't know how you get away from that. As much as you try to protect yourself from everything that happens in the world, and in your family and in yourself. You can't get away from it. Life happens.

But when life happens, you stick by one another. This is home. This is where your support is.

Adam is the eternal optimist. I think that's what has kept it going for me. I feel so incredibly unlovable sometimes. I think we all do. But I don't think Adam does. He just says things like, "What are you talking about? We're fine. I'll always love you."

She has a lot more ups and downs than I do.

Do I? That's probably why my therapy bills are higher. It's true. Adam is more level. But maybe that's why we work! I have the ups and downs and he just plows through.

She gets more excited and she gets more worried.

The highs and the lows are higher and lower that's for sure. That's the beauty of estrogen. Thank god for estrogen.

I wouldn't know.

Never in my whole life have I ever met somebody who is so giving. I couldn't even believe that he was so giving, and so genuine and so kind to my kids and my family. How could I not marry him? And for some reason he stayed.

She was willing.

He had me in the shower. I couldn't have said no.

HOW TO MARRY THE MAN OF

YOUR CHOICE

(WITHIN A YEAR)

Bethany, 53

Chris, 59

married 23 years

As I walk up the gravel driveway underneath a canopy of trees, I feel as if I am in the middle of a mythical forest and this house is something out of a storybook. I ring the doorbell and am met by an old, wheezing black Labrador with a white beard. "Oh don't mind Missy," Bethany says, "She'll just slobber all over you, but she's harmless." As I walk up the stairs to the bright, open living room, Chris opens the sliding glass door and steps inside, covered with what looks like soot. "Sorry! I was working in the backyard. I'll be down in a minute." Bethany pours some iced tea as she explains, "Chris is a blacksmith. He's always working on stuff back there. I've stopped asking questions and just let him go…so, wait, what is this interview about exactly?"

My name is Bethany, I'm fifty-three and I've been married twenty-three years. My husband's name is Chris.

And I'm fifty-nine.

I was twenty-eight years old when we met. I had been working in Boston with Chris's sister. She and I had worked together for about a year and then I moved to a small university in Maine to be a professor there. So I was living in Maine and I was invited down for her surprise birthday party in January. And her brother, Chris, was in town training for his job.

I have this really vivid memory of walking up to the house. There was this big glass window and I could see a man on the other side of it. Now I knew that I would know everyone at this party, and I didn't know who this person was. I was really intrigued. You know how you can sort of watch someone from afar and get their non-verbal's? I thought to myself, "Hmmm, he's good looking, he seems comfortable and he has a nice smile..." Let's just say, I was intrigued.

We did a lot of talking that evening and I told her that I was going to be in Boston for two weeks.

So I made the excuse to go down and visit his sister a couple of times.

I had that following weekend off before flying home.

And I suggested that he come to Maine, since he had never been to Maine before. Which was really sort of, I don't know, it felt very bold.

So I did! We had a great time. We hit it off right away and we realized we liked a lot of similar things. But, unfortunately I was engaged at the time to someone else.

His family didn't like this woman at <u>all</u>. And, being such good friends with his sister, I knew his parents very well. So when they realized that there was this spark between us, they were quite invested in supporting that.

I obviously broke off the engagement pretty quickly after that.

Then we dated for a year and a half, long distance. I was in Maine and he was in Indiana. We talked a lot about who was going to move and at that point in time I was more flexible, so we got married and I moved to Indiana.

Now that I think about it, it was such a risk. We had never lived together. I had lived with another boyfriend previous to that for a couple of years and I knew it wasn't right. I knew I didn't want to take the next step. But with Chris, I just knew. I was really ready. I felt that it was right. I remember when I was little I would ask my mom, "How did you know that dad was the right person to marry?" And her answer would seem so unsatisfactory: "You just know." I would get so annoyed. "But <u>how</u> do you know?" And honestly, I just knew. I knew with Chris almost immediately.

Well, she was thirty and I was thirty-six. We had lived, we knew who we were. Sometimes I think when people get married very young, you grow and change and sometimes you grow and change in a different way. We were very solid in who we were and where we were going by that time.

It's funny, as you get closer to thirty, especially women, you get anxious. You think, "Oh I've got to get married" or, "I have to have children" and all of that. I was certainly feeling that. My father actually sent me this book. It was hysterical. He was anxious that I wasn't getting married, and he sent me this book titled, "How to

Marry The Man of Your Choice Within a Year." It was like, where did he even find this? And why would he go through all this trouble to send it to me? I guess the message he was trying to send was pretty clear: "Come on already! Figure it out!!"

It is so funny to have that external social pressure to get married. Like we don't put enough pressure on ourselves already.

Chris proposed to me in October (we met in January), so dad was happy about that. I was visiting him in Indiana and hoped this might happen. We were just hanging out at his house when he asked me to marry him. I said yes without hesitation. Later that evening we celebrated with a dinner, Chris booked this little nook that only had one or two tables in it, so it was very private and romantic. He got down on one knee at the restaurant and re-proposed properly to me there.

We looked for an engagement ring a month later when I came to visit Bethany in Maine.

I just wanted a simple sapphire and diamond ring, nothing large, flashy or expensive. And I still have it to this day.

We got married the following June in my hometown of Clinton, New York. We thought it would be a good halfway point for his friends and family from Indiana and my friends and family from the east coast. We were married in the same church that my parents were married in and had the reception at my parent's home. Clinton is a small town and my parents lived in the country, so we had two large tents set up on their lawn. One for food and one for the band and dancing. We kept it really simple. My sister and I did all the flowers for the church, the tables, bouquets, my hair...it was so much fun! It was a lovely afternoon reception with champagne and food that we had catered in. Our only splurge was to have a live band for dancing.

And then we went on our honeymoon.

I had a tiny little beach house in Maine, so we went there. Then we went up to Bar Harbor and Arcadia National Park. We went hiking and played in the ocean. We've gone on some really nice vacations since then. We're really good at traveling together.

And we are still so active together. I think that's really important, to be active and be present in the world together.

For our anniversary this year, we got stand up paddleboards and went up to our cottage to celebrate. Some people our age are like, "Oh, be careful! Can you do that? Isn't it hard?" And it's like, no it's not that hard. But just to be able to take that physical risk together is important. I think when people get in their fifties and stuff they take less of those risks. But that's what life's about! Having fun and taking risks.

I think what has really made us reflect in the last three years is that we've lost three of our four parents. So there has been a lot of reflection on what do we want out of life? Where do we want to go? Where do we see ourselves? And through that reflection we actually ended up buying this cottage up north. It has been so much fun to do that together and to play up there together. We've fixed it up. It's been a new project that we've done together. I think that it's important to have those types of projects. To figure out how to negotiate those things and dream together.

We actually designed our house together and built it.

That was a big project. I was the principle builder on

it. It took forever but it was worth it I think.

That was a hard time for us. We were both so busy and we lived in our own worlds for a while. Sheila was born and I think I felt very much like a single parent at times. When the kids are little and you're not getting any sleep, it's hard to have time for a relationship. Or there were times when I was doing my doctoral program and working full time, and Chris was developing his business. It felt like we were ships passing in the night. And it's not that we didn't still love each other, but it was a different time in our lives.

I think what has been really wonderful is we've sort of come out the other end now. We don't have any kids at home and it's fun to rediscover that we actually have fun together!

Chris just makes me laugh. We like so many similar things. It's really nice to realize, "Oh yeah, that's why I married you." I think at some point, you as an individual have to decide to recommit to a relationship. Because it does get difficult after a while. I think some people decide not to recommit. And that's their choice. But I certainly think that we did and I'm happy we did because being with Chris is so much fun.

I think that ebb and flow stuff is really hard. Sometimes it's like, "Hmm, do I really want this still?" But if you really look at it and try to figure it out together, that's special.

The biggest choice, the biggest, single choice in your life, is who you get married to. And when you're young I guess you don't really consider that. But now, being older, you really see how true it is.

Well, you marry your best friend.

I always think about the incredible trust I have with Chris. I really trust him. If something was wrong, or if there was some apocalypse or something, I'd want to be with him because he can figure things out. And I think we'd get through it. To have that kind of trust and faith in one another is really pretty amazing.

I feel like it's the day-to-day things that I find fulfillment in. The day-to-day pleasure that I find in doing things with Bethany such as walking down to the market together. I derive a lot of pleasure and enjoyment from those little things.

It was cute earlier, about an hour ago, I was working on the computer and I wanted to tell Chris something so I went outside. As I was about to go back in he said, "Hold on, make a pot of coffee and I'll come sit down and have some with you." So we were sitting out on the back patio. And as we were drinking our coffee he suddenly said, "I love sitting here talking to you." And the feeling is just so mutual!

Well that's good. If it wasn't, I'd be in trouble I guess!

ANNA BOWEN

HOME

Betty, 69

married 50 years to Greg, deceased.

I've lived up the street from Grandma Betty for as long as I can remember. Although she's not my real grandmother, Betty took care of all the kids in our neighborhood. Pictures of the neighbors and their children cover her walls. Knick-knacks of angelic cherubs and porcelain kittens sit on shelves in the kitchen. Homemade macadamia nut cookies sit in a Tupperware container on the stove. Although I've lived next door to Betty for most of my life, this is the very first time I have ever been inside her home.

Hello, my name is Betty and I am sixty-nine years old. Greg and I were married for fifty years. I was nineteen when we got married and he turned twenty right after the wedding.

I met him at a drive-in on Stadium Boulevard. It was "Everett's Drive-In." It was a hamburger place. One of the first that had the little phones you could call and make your orders and stuff. I was still in high school. And he was just out of high school. Oh my, guys used to drive their cars around and around. They'd all go drag racing on Stadium Boulevard, and hopefully not get caught. The girls weren't allowed in the cars. Excess weight you know. We would just watch. They'd spin out, showing how big and bad they were. A lot of girls liked the cars. That was our big thing at that time. So that's where I met him. A friend introduced us and then we went to her house. The boys followed us, and that was that! I was a senior in high school. So I was just seventeen.

I think our first actual "date" was also at the drive-in. Got a burger, came home, and that was it. Then every Friday night we'd either go to a movie at the drive-in or to somebody's house. Not much else to do. It was kind of quiet I guess. Although they used to have parking lot dances on the top of the parking structure in the summertime. They'd have a DJ and it was free. There was pop and stuff to eat. It was just a place where you could go, you know.

But that was about it. That was all they had unless you were involved in after school sports or something. Which they didn't have that much of either. It was just a different time.

So we had been dating for about a year and we were at my house. My mom and dad had gone to a party that night and we were watching my nephew. And that's where Greg proposed. I think he had said something to my dad beforehand. It was good. It was nice. It was just the way it was. What can I say…it wasn't really romantic or anything. It was just what people did. I still have the same ring. I never did get another one. Fifty-one years old. It's getting thin.

We got married in a Catholic church. I had a short dress. I didn't want a long one. It was mid calf. It was hotter than hot. June. We had a hundred and twenty-five, maybe a hundred and fifty people there. Which, when you're nineteen, looking down that big, fat, aisle, it's like, "What am I doing here?" It was scary, but it was what I wanted because all of our friends were the same way. Everybody got out of school, got married and had kids. Daddy worked and mom stayed home. That was the way it was. And that's what we did.

At that time I worked downtown at what was called "The Marilyn Shop." It was a college shop that had dyed-to-match sets. Like, you would have a powder blue tight skirt and a powder blue sweater, and they would match. It was the thing for college girls in those days. That was down on campus.

But then I got pregnant with Mitchell and after a while I had to quit. We lived about twenty minutes from downtown. The street where we lived is pretty popular now. It's got a bar and stuff on it. But at that time it was out in the country. A family had broken up their old farmland and built these duplexes that we rented for sixty-five dollars a month. And it was nice! It was one bedroom but it was a really nice place.

So then Mitch was born and Greg and I looked for another place to live. We lived with Greg's parents for a bit, and then we moved into another duplex on the other side of town where we had Christine. We had three bedrooms and I think it was a hundred and twenty-five a month.

Then we started looking for a house and these houses were just being built. So we looked here and here we are. I liked this one *because it was so close to the school. The kids could walk home for lunch. It was a no-brainer. We were the first ones to own a house on this street.*

I was fortunate enough to stay home with the kids. I didn't work till they were in high school. A lot of people don't realize what they've got in their kids. They set 'em in front of the TV, give 'em their games, and let 'em go…and you miss so much if you do that.

Our daughter Christine passed away some years ago now. Greg was laid off, so he was able to be with her in those last three years. He was able to take her to all of her doctor's appointments and stuff. He was able to be with her. I remember she said to me once, she said, "Mom, that's the dad I never knew I had." So a good thing can come from a bad thing I guess. In those last years she had, oh golly, she had kidney transplants, an amputation, and all this stuff.

That's the hardest. To lose a child. I mean you go through deaths. I recently lost Greg to cancer. My parents passed away some time ago now. And I also took care of my sister until she died. But that's different. It's sad, but it's different. You're not meant to bury a child. It's something you never expect.

I was at work when it happened. I was trying to teach somebody how to do something, and Mitch called me. I said, "No, no, no, that's not true. Somebody's playing a joke." Till finally, it was. It was true. And you work through the pain, but Greg was my rock.

Greg and I were opposite. Which is why I think it worked. We were complete opposites. He was very quiet. He was social at times, but I really put myself out there. I'm the one with the mouth. He would just come home from work and eat and do his thing…

But that was just what husbands and dads did. Nowadays I

ANNA BOWEN

*guess they work on the computer. But honestly, if we ever got into an
argument, a serious one, he would just clam up, turn around, and
walk away until I got under control. Then we could talk about it.
And that's how we worked through everything. We would just talk
it out. But it took us a while to get there 'cause I like to hash it out.
Let's do it now!*

*I've seen so many other relationships fall apart. Nobody's
willing to fight anymore for what they want. And I understand a lot
of that, or cheating or lying, that's totally different. But nit-pickin' is
what a lot of our friends did, 'cause it was easy to get a divorce.
Very few of my friends are still married. Two, I think, that I can
name.*

*I've thought about remarrying but honestly I have such a
wonderful life. I feel so fulfilled and happy. I learned so much
patience from being with Greg. I became more patient than I ever
was. I'm just generally mellowed more. I go with the flow now, so I
suppose if someone else came along, I'd be open to it.*

*I hope I age gracefully. You know you get to this age and it's
like, do I want to sell my house? Do I want to move? Do I want to
live in a condo? And then it's like, "Okay, if I move from here
where would I go?" I've been here for so long, I don't know where
I'd go. Here, you can walk downtown if you want to, and the bus
line's right there if you need it. The only thing is that blasted hill.
That's the kicker. But there's no other place that I can think of
that I want to go but here. This is home.*

*But it's the stuff! Oh my gosh, I've got all our stuff, all of our
parent's stuff. I still have some of the kid's stuff and it's like,
"Okay what do I _do_ with all this?" I've got records of my dad's,
'78's. Well, what am I supposed to do with those? And why on
earth am I hanging on to them?*

I guess I have to go through it before I can't anymore. But it's a hard decision. What to throw away, and what to keep.

ANNA BOWEN

A GOOD HUNCH

Geena, 62

Jim, 62

married 10 years

As I enter Geena and Jim's beautiful home I am met with the hearty, comforting aroma of homemade soup simmering on the stove. "We made you dinner!" Geena exclaims excitedly. "I hope you're not a vegetarian!" An assortment of African and Japanese kabuki masks decorate the mantel around the fireplace where a roaring fire crackles. Microphones, keyboards, and guitars are all set up for a rehearsal that the couple has later in the evening with their band.

I'm Geena and I'm 62.

I'm Jim and I'm 62.

We have been married for ten years and together for twelve. But we've known each other since high school.

Mrs. Kelly's freshman English class…

We met in the 60's when all of the folk and protest music was really raging. We formed a band and played music together almost every day. After school Jimmy would bring his guitar over. He kind of became like the forth kid in our family. We have pictures of him decorating our Christmas tree all throughout high school. The four of us were great friends. My sister, my brother, Jimmy and me.

After high school I worked for Geena's dad. He was a construction superintendent and during the summers I would work with him. After work we'd head on over to their house where we'd drink Jim Beam and play music all night long.

The late sixties and early seventies was a great time.

Our parents were all musicians and were all very close. So we would play music together all the time, have dinners at each other's houses and spend the holidays together.

We never dated though.

Well, I asked her to the prom but she didn't want to go.

It wasn't because I didn't want to go with him…I just thought school dances were stupid.

I didn't take it personally.

So even though we were kids together and we liked each other, there was never a romantic connection. And as the years went by, I stayed here in town, got married and had kids.

And I moved all around the country and became involved in other relationships. I was married twice. When I was twenty-two, I married a woman who had three boys and was six years older than me. That lasted for thirteen years. My folks were not thrilled about that relationship to say the least. But I was so young. I just didn't know what I wanted. After about ten years, I began to realize the relationship was not healthy for me. I ended it, and a few years later I met someone else. I was married to this other woman for six years. Although she was a very dear person, she was not a very happy person. She had a couple of screws loose that she wasn't looking to tighten any time soon. The fact that she fell in love with her boss and left me was a blessing. She ended our relationship, but I would have taken measures to leave if she hadn't taken the initiative.

I got married when I was thirty-two and was married for ten years. My former husband was a great guy. We had so much in common. We talked all the time about politics and art and music. I had two fabulous kids with him. Although we cared about each other very much, it just didn't work in terms of a long-term marriage. But we are still very good friends. He is still involved with our children and is very much a part of my life.

Throughout our other relationships and marriages, Geena and I always stayed in touch. I would see her when I came home to visit my folks. We still had Thanksgivings and Christmases together and all of that.

Then in 1998 we decided to go to our 30th high school reunion together.

And from that year on, things started to change. We really started to make more of an effort to keep in touch. My dad passed away in 1999 so Geena helped me through that…

Then in the year 2000, we were both nearing our fiftieth birthdays, and my daughter was graduating high school. After her graduation ceremony, we had a big party at my house. I think of that night as our first date.

The tide turned that evening for sure. I crashed on a lounge chair in Geena's living room and she put a blanket over me. I remember waking up at 6 am, flying home and thinking to myself, "Something is different." After I got back home, we began to talk on the phone every night. And we both came to the conclusion that we wanted to pursue this. We wanted to explore the possibility of a relationship.

It was kind of weird though. I mean we had known each other for almost forty years! We were both thinking, "Okay, are we going to blow this friendship?"

It was a risk for sure. We knew our friendship had always been strong and we were willing to risk that by seeing if there was something else there. We were both really tentative but we soon realized that it was going to work!

It was a big deal the first time I flew out to spend the weekend with him. This was about a month after my daughter's graduation.

When I came to pick Geena up at the airport she was

wearing jeans, a white oxford shirt and a tweed blazer. She was so beautiful. I remember thinking to myself, "This is the deal. This is it. This is the end of this searching that my life has been about."

We spent that weekend walking around town, eating in fabulous places, talking and drinking wine. And that was that! We knew it was right. It was the perfect time for us to get together. In all the years we had known one another, we had always been involved with other people or involved with our own lives…we didn't have time to think about having a relationship. But he wasn't just my good friend Jimmy any longer. There was chemistry that happened between us because we were finally ready.

We were in a long distance relationship for about six months. Every couple of weeks or so one of us would fly out and visit the other. Then I moved back to our hometown, where Geena had been all along, and we decided to live together. About a year later we began to discuss marriage. It was more my idea than hers.

Definitely. I had no intention of ever marrying again. I didn't really see the point. I had always been in charge of my life and I had never been dependant on anyone. But because it was Jimmy, I began to change my mind. Because we had known each other for so long, and he was such a part of my family already, there was a comfort level between us that was so natural. It soon became apparent that marriage was the right path.

So we got married at the "Neighborhood Church" in the pastor's chamber. It was just immediate family.

It was really important to me to keep it small and private. And then we came back to our house and had a big party!

Being with Geena differed greatly from my previous

relationships. And I think a lot of that had to do with age. I had always been with people who were much older than I was or much younger. Although there were other disconnects in those relationships besides age, I do believe human beings that are the same age often have more in common. Geena and I were in similar places in our lives when we got married. Even though we had taken different paths, we had gone through similar phases and had similar outlooks on life. To me that was huge. And it was so different from my past experiences.

I have always felt so comfortable with Jimmy because there is so much about him that makes me feel absolutely at ease. The music thing is really an incredible connection we have. Music is so important to both of us and to our families. But Jimmy is also creative in other ways. He builds things and makes things and I absolutely love that. He is always working on projects and he always has something on the horizon. He really is like my father in that way.

I think a lot of the attributes that we like about each other are attributes that our parents had: Music, building, fixing and creating. Our parents were all very creative and I think that's why Geena and I are attracted to the same things. It isn't surprising to me that we have so much in common. I had a good hunch on that plane ride back home. I remember thinking, "If not now...when?"

We've only been married for ten years and yet we have a fifty-year relationship. There is a depth between us that ten years wouldn't even begin to describe!

We really feel like we're a family. We are so committed to one another and we respect each other so much. Of course, like any couple, we have our ups and downs. We have little fights here and there. But we don't really have any major disagreements.

One of the things we have had to adjust to is the way we deal with one another when we are upset. Jimmy likes to talk things through and process things right away, and I usually need space and time to cool down.

Over time I came to learn that Geena is much more comfortable letting the dust settle before we talk about things. It was hard for me at first but I came to realize that things worked out better for us when we did wait. And it took the pressure off of me to try and figure things out right away.

Respecting how your partner needs to handle something is really important. There is something really soothing and supportive in that. But we respect each other so much that we rarely have major arguments. We are always very polite to one another. We never shout when we are angry or upset. That does not happen. You don't treat a person you love in a disrespectful way. That's just not part of who we are.

I've been in relationships that had a real combative edge to them; filled with altercations that were usually induced by alcohol. Those types of relationships never serve you well.

But honestly, we haven't had to go through many hardships in the ten years we've been together, and we really don't get into too many fights.

Yes, these past ten years have been very smooth. We haven't lost anyone, and we've been very healthy, which we don't take for granted.

Jimmy and I both know hardship, and we feel very fortunate that together we have not had to shoulder anything huge yet. I lost both of my parents when I was in my late thirties so I went through that before Jimmy and I got together. Jimmy lost his father before we were together as well and had some health issues when he was in his forties. But luckily (knock on wood) we are both healthy and happy now! Of course we know hardships will come. We're not Pollyanna. Yes, life happens and difficulties come about. But we really have not had to face many challenges in the time that we have been together.

I think our biggest challenges so far have come with raising our kids. When our kids go through rough spots sometimes there is nothing we can do. And that is hard. In my life there has been nothing more difficult than seeing my kids unhappy. No matter how much we try to smooth the way, we can't prepare them for everything.

Aside from the fabulous person Jimmy is, he is also a wonderful father to my kids. To our kids. There would have been no way this relationship could have happened if that wasn't an aspect of his character. Part of my identity is being a mother.

You know, love is a funny word. It takes on so many different meanings…

It almost seems silly to say, "Oh, we're together because we love each other…" It sounds too simple in a way. It sounds too common.

I mean what is the definition of love, really?

Well…that's kind of what we've been talking about I guess!

ANNA BOWEN

IRENE AND RED

Jean, 50

Richard, 56

married 24 years

*As I walk into Jean and Richard's home, I'm greeted by an old
yellow Labrador and a feisty dachshund. A small cat rubs up
against my legs as both dogs scramble around to fight for my
attention. "You guys have no shame." Richard chuckles. "I guess
they're starved for attention." Richard makes violins in his
workshop (the garage) and all sorts of stringed instruments decorate
the walls. As I sit and ready myself for the interview by the bay
window, their dachshund, Louie, jumps onto my lap and makes
himself at home.*

I'm Jean. I am fifty years old…and…I have no idea how long I've been married.

Twenty-four years. I'm Richard…and I'm twenty-one years old! No, just kidding. I'm fifty-six.

Richard and I moved to the city around the same time and I lived in an apartment complex downtown. I met some people who lived below me and worked with Richard. They kept saying they knew this really great guy who had just moved to town, but I wasn't really ready to date at that time. I was getting out of a horrible relationship. But Richard started hanging out at the apartment and we would go bowling together as a group on Saturday nights. We all made up fake names and the rule was, we couldn't talk about work. I was twenty-four. And my name was Irene.

My name was Red. My beard was red at that time.

Not anymore! He's grey now.

Thanks honey…

So we would all have a beer and bowl and have these kind of different personalities. It was really fun.

It was cool. Nobody could complain about work because we weren't allowed to talk about it!

So basically, these people set us up. They told me that Richard had low blood sugar.

Which I did.

Which he did. And I was a nurse working over at the hospital. So I said, "You have to fast all night and in the morning come over and I'll check your blood sugar." Well he came over the next morning and I checked his blood sugar, which was low of course, and then he took me to breakfast. And that was that! That was our first date! We were together from then on.

We both knew we wanted to be together so there was no official engagement. It was never, "Do you wanna?" it was, "When do you wanna?" We started living together very soon after we started dating. We just got along really well. It sounds silly, but sometimes you just know when you meet the right person.

There wasn't a formal engagement or even a ring. We were broke. We ended up going to some store and buying the cheapest rings we could get.

Still got it! She's got a fancy one now though.

Because it was his grandma's! But I don't ever recall a proposal. We just knew.

Here's the big news: I was still technically married to someone else while I was engaged to Jean. It took me almost four years to get divorced. I had been married for seven years and was separated for three at that time. I was twenty-three when I got married. I was too young. And it was a nightmare getting divorced because my ex was not very easy to deal with. She was constantly sending her lawyer after me and I was constantly sending the same letter back saying, "Okay, you can have this and that." It was horrible.

We were planning our wedding and he still wasn't divorced yet! I was just like, "Well, hopefully this wedding will happen!"

My first wife was very difficult. She's an artist. I'm not a psychology major or anything but she had kind of a weak father. He was a very nice guy and a wonderfully smart man, but the mom ran the household and he didn't ever really stand up for himself. So I think she expected our relationship to be similar. Everything that went wrong was somehow my fault. That's a lot of responsibility to have! I just couldn't deal with it. She was jealous as well. I was having a lot of success creatively and she wasn't. She would do destructive things and sabotage my stuff. But even through all of that, we didn't give up. We went to therapy and did all sorts of stuff. I soon realized that I would never have a healthy relationship with this woman, so I had to cut it off. Jean and I were waiting and waiting for the papers to go through and they never did. Finally, I had to countersue to get divorced. It was rough.

It's funny because he never thought he was going to get married again.

Well I never thought I was going to meet anybody that I would like again because I had been through three years of hell.

But then he met me!

We had the wedding at a little church out of town. We knew the minister because he had married some friends of ours and we thought he had done a great job. We really just wanted to get our two families together. It wasn't a large wedding. Eighty people tops.

My brother wore a kilt.

And he played the bagpipes. She's Scottish so we had to have bagpipes of course. My son, Scott, was the ring bearer. He was seven at the time. And my sister was the flower girl. It was a nice wedding. Then we put a volleyball net up in the front of the church, a tent in the back, and we catered in.

We brought our stereo system and had some mixed tapes.

The invitation said: Bring your jeans! So after the wedding, people changed into their jeans and played volleyball. It was great. I had more fun at my wedding than I have ever had at any party.

And then we went camping for our honeymoon…because we had no money. It was beautiful though. It was a perfect, perfect honeymoon. Just simple and fun. Then I got pregnant within that first year. We wanted to have kids right away.

I got custody of Scott pretty soon after we were married. Originally my ex-wife got custody of him. I said, "Fine, I get him all summer and I want him on holidays," you know, that kind of stuff. But I knew my ex really well and I knew once he hit age ten she wasn't going to be able to handle him.

I remember Richard telling me that and thinking to myself, how could you not <u>handle</u> your own son? It made no sense to me.

I was right though! He turned ten, my ex-wife called me and said, "I can't handle him." And I said, "Send him on over."

So Scott moved in with us after our daughter Cynthia was a year old. And he lived with us till he was about sixteen. That was hard. It was tough on him and tough on us. I was in my twenties and I was the parent of a one-year-old. I didn't know how to be a parent of a teenager. And in Scott's mind, you know he was only ten, so he thought he was just going to get to hang out with his dad. He thought his mom and dad were going to get back together eventually. It wasn't his fault they split up. It's never the kid's fault. I just felt like my role was to nurture him, but not be his mother because I could never replace her. But it was hard for him. We had different rules than she had. Living in two different households is tough for kids. In retrospect, there are things I would've done differently in terms of being a parent. I was pretty intense with Scott and I had expectations that were probably unrealistic. I just didn't know anything about teenagers.

He wasn't an easy kid either. He was very creative but he tested us all the time. I remember he came home with blue hair once, trying to freak me out. But with my childhood, there's no way you could mess with me. I don't think he could've done anything worse than I did when I was a kid. So he showed up with this wild haircut, I think someone had just sheared off places on his head, and this blue hair dye that he had put on in a McDonald's bathroom. He walked in the door with his buddies, I was doing the dishes, and I looked up over my glasses and said, "Oh, nice haircut. You look like grandma." And I went back to doing the dishes.

Well, it's about picking your battles. We couldn't have cared less about blue hair.

And frankly, I could pick my battles. But the hard part was that I was gone a lot for work and that's when he acted out the most.

I was at home with my little one and I just didn't know what to do.

I spent long hours on the phone in different time zones talking to principles and stuff. It was bad.

I was tough as a kid. I was a really tough teenager. I did a lot of drugs. I ran away from home…I put my parents through a lot. So that was hard because I was looking at this young guy growing into his teenage body and I'm thinking, "What do I do as a parent to stop this?" And I had to learn that sometimes there's not anything you can do. Sometimes you just have to love them and be as patient as you can. And he turned out fine. Sometimes it just takes time. Every kid is different.

Hey, he only spent a week in jail! That was the point in which he had to grow up and figure out some stuff. From that point on, he straightened out. And now he's doing fine.

Deep down we knew Scott was a really good guy. He was a good kid and he would never physically or emotionally hurt anybody. He just got in with the wrong crowd and the wrong situation. He's in his thirties now and has his own little guy. But Richard and I certainly went through time periods where we wondered if we were going to stay together. We fought a lot during those years.

Raising kids is really hard.

When the kids were little, Richard was traveling all the time and we didn't have health insurance, so we were trying to figure that out. Money was always an issue.

But the time passes. You work it out. After a while I actually decided to quit my job and work from home. That was really great. I became the main breadwinner and the stay at home dad all in one! Leaving that company was one of the best things I ever did.

And it worked out because I could go back to work!

We've had to work on our relationship a lot. We have a lot of friends who have ended up divorced. It seems like they stopped having fun a long time ago and forgot that they even liked each other once. There was nothing to save when all was said and done. I feel like it's important to work through the hard parts because you have fun other times.

And that's what we have is a lot of fun. We play board games, we hang out with our friends, we go out and listen to music and dance. That's what life is about.

We still talk late at night till two or three in the morning.

Sometimes it's about intense stuff that we need to talk about, but a lot of times we'll just talk about anything. We're such good friends. That's key in a good, solid relationship. I don't like Richard all the time, but I love him. Friends don't always have to like each other.

Usually when I can't stand her, she's just being a good mirror. Making me see myself.

And he's eased up. Thank god.

Well now wait a second. I'm a very goal oriented person and I've gotten what I wanted because I'm stubborn and I never gave up. I am an artist. And for people who aren't artists, well, we can be very hard to take. It took me a while to figure out that there are other perspectives out there and other ways of living life.

Richard was very stubborn when we first met and still is to some degree, but he's more facilitating and now he's not as "busy" all the time. He's definitely mellowed out as he's gotten older. And I'm not as intense either. I think a huge thing that has helped us move forward is that Richard can also admit, as he's gotten older, when he's wrong. I think in general it's very hard for men to admit when they're wrong.

I'm never wrong! Kidding. I'm kidding.

I've also had some hardships in my life and I knew Richard would always stick with me no matter what. I knew that it could get really bad and he'd always be there for me. And that's a really good place to be.

There's a good part of stubborn, called loyal.

That loyalty is huge. One of the hardest times in our relationship was when I was going through some intense therapy and realized that my grandfather had sexually abused me as a child. There were some repressed memories that came flooding back to me. During that time Richard couldn't come near me. I pushed him away because I was dealing with my own pain and trying to figure all of this stuff out. That took us to another level of our relationship because he stood by me the entire time. He was there for me even at a time when I wasn't able to meet any of his needs. And I don't even mean sexually. Emotionally I was not there for him at all. But knowing he was there for me allowed me to go through my pain and heal. I don't think I could've done that by myself. It was too huge. I was so depressed and it was affecting so many parts of my life. If Richard wasn't there for me I think I would've chosen not to deal with my pain. If he wasn't there, I may have said, "You know what? I'm not going to deal with this. I'm just going to tuck it back in my brain and forget about it." But he provided a safe environment for me to face and work through things. It took about two years to work through it all.

That was challenging.

Oh yeah, it was huge. But I fell in love with him even more then because he was there. He stuck by my side.

Yeah...that was challenging...I don't think I'd like to relive that. Sometimes when you're going through stuff, you just have to work through it and get it out of your system. You have to have whatever emotions you're going to have about it and come through the other side. Of course Jean was dealing with it her way, and I was looking for an elephant gun that I could shoot the problem with. That was not an easy time. But I hardly remember it now. That was about fifteen years ago.

I know, it's so bizarre. It feels like it was so long ago. We've been together a long time honey.

God, you're old.

So are you!

And I still like you! What's that about?

I still like you too! I think another thing that keeps our relationship healthy is that we also have our own separate lives. I have my own friends, women friends, that I do things with and go on trips with, and he has things that he does. It's funny, some people at work will say to me, "Does your husband mind that you're doing this without him?" Number one, no he doesn't mind and number two? That's not even a part of our relationship. I don't need permission to have this other part of my life, and neither does he. I think that has really enriched us as we've gotten older. We know people who don't have separate lives and who don't do separate things. But we encourage that in each other. We want to have our own lives. I think it makes us stronger as a couple, I really do.

We just get along. We get each other. We like the same things but we like different things too. She's a very different person than I am but that doesn't mean I don't appreciate who she is.

I pull him way outside of his box.

And I do the same thing to her.

He does!

I think we just want similar things out of life. Needs are relatively simple. It's really great when you have extra stuff, but it's not necessary.

It's not about having things for us. We like to travel. Travel's big for us.

When we retire we're looking at those mini trailers, you know? The ones that you can pull behind a jeep?

We want to go to all the national parks. We would love to do that. For us that would be the perfect way to retire. Both of our girls are in college now and Scott is all grown up, so all of a sudden we have an empty house. For a minute I wondered if it was going to be difficult with just the two of us. Having kids in the house is a major distraction.

To me it's a non-issue. It's just really quiet. That's the only thing I notice.

Maybe we should get more pets!

<u>No</u>.

PLAYING HOUSE

Lynne, 50

Paul, 58

married 26 years

This was my first interview, and is very near and dear to my heart.

My name is Lynne and this is Paul. We've been married for twenty-six years. I'm fifty and he's fifty-eight.

That's right. I'll be fifty-nine in a few weeks

And I'll be fifty-one in a month. We met at a mutual friend's daughter's first birthday party. That's when we first saw each other. I was there with my two-year-old daughter and Paul was there with his girlfriend who looked rather uncomfortable. There were a lot of single moms with babies there and she was a "fine, upstanding woman."

There were just no little children in our lives, so she didn't know what to do.

Then Paul said he was going to scrape off the windshield of their car before they left and I called out, "You can scrape off my windshield anytime!" I guess that was kind of obnoxious but he must've thought it was cute...I was twenty-two or twenty-three. I was just being silly.

Well my impression of our first meeting goes something like this: I was there with my girlfriend, we were breaking up at that time but she still came along with me to keep me company. I had not met Lynne before, but I was really taken by her and her daughter, Lakisha. Lakisha was just as cute as a button and super energetic. She was hopping around and playing with all the other kids. She was calling me "My Paul" by the end of the night. And of course I noticed that Lynne was stunningly beautiful.

Oh! He had a really nice butt back then and so did I. That's what he told me later that attracted him to me the most was my butt.

Yeah that was true. Lynne's bottom was really outstanding. In any case, I remembered her and as the relationship with my girlfriend unwound, I got to the point where I wanted to meet other people…so I asked our friend about Lynne.

I had actually asked our friend earlier about Paul. I said that I didn't think that square woman was right for him and I thought I would be. So she had Paul and I both over for dinner a few weeks later, and afterwards Paul asked me out!

We went to a little restaurant in Ypsilanti.

"Aubrey's."

No it wasn't "Aubrey's," it was a little restaurant. It's not there anymore. That's how long ago this was.

What was it called? No, it <u>was</u> "Aubrey's."

No it <u>wasn't</u> "Aubrey's." It was in a little hotel. I can't remember what it was called.

So then we started talking and I began talking about Lakisha. Then I was like, "Oh, sorry, I'm not going to talk about Lakisha right now because this is a first date and I'm supposed to talk about me and my stuff." And Paul was like, "That's okay, Lakisha's a big part of your life and I don't mind if you talk about her." That made me feel good…because I really didn't have much else to talk about.

We had a nice conversation. Lynne was very…

Hungry!

Well she was very real. I liked the fact that she had a large meal. A lot of the women I had been dating were kind of, oh how should I describe it…they would get a salad or something. White wine and salad.

But I was really hungry so I got a steak and a baked potato. Hey, I knew someone else was paying for it!

She was refreshing. She did not seem to be worried about anything. I told her to order whatever she wanted and she did.

I really did. Then on our next date we included Lakisha and went roller-skating. Lakisha didn't like roller-skating so she took off her skates and ran around the rink with her tennis shoes on. We got in trouble.

Lakisha wasn't afraid of anything. She decided roller-skating didn't work so she said to me, "I'll roller-skate <u>without</u> skates!" Well, that logic couldn't be denied. I said, "Okay, Lakisha. If you want to roller-skate without skates, that's just fine." They didn't let us do it, but I liked that about Lakisha. She was a kid who wanted to have fun and if something didn't feel right, then she wasn't going to do it. That was okay by me.

We dated for about nine months before he proposed. But about three months in he asked me if I would hypothetically marry him. He had dated other women before me obviously but whenever the idea of marriage came up they wouldn't want to commit. So he wanted to know ahead of time if I was really interested and where this relationship could go. Not that it would go there…but hypothetically. He said, "Hey, Lynne, would you marry me? Hypothetically?" And I said, "Yeah, I guess so." But we had probably consumed like three or four drinks so I didn't take the question very seriously.

In my past relationships, I never really started out

thinking about marriage. But in our case, I thought about marriage right away. It was simple. Lynne seemed like a really special person and I thought I could easily be married to her. There were so many qualities about her that I wanted to have in my wife and in my partner. And as I got to know her better it didn't take me long to see where this could go. A lot of the people I dated in the past were fun to be with, but there were differences in our personalities that made me wonder how long we would last. It just so happened I knew what I was looking for. I didn't know if I was going to find it, but when I found Lynne, I knew she was the one for me and I wanted to let her know what my intentions were. But, you see, it wasn't just Lynne I had to consider. It was Lakisha. Lakisha was ready for a dad. I wanted to give her that. I wanted to settle down and make our family legit.

There are a couple of things that I haven't mentioned yet about my first impressions of Paul. Because he had offered to scrape off that woman's car that night at the party I knew he took care of people. I hadn't really had that in my life and that was really important to me. Not that I knew what I was looking for in a man. I just wanted to be with somebody who was nice to me. I guess I had pretty low expectations. Paul ended up being way, way more than I ever could have hoped for. I remember there was a time when Paul called me, we had gone out every single weekend for several weeks in a row, and he called me at work and said, "I wanted to let you know that I have plans this weekend both Friday and Saturday. I know that we've been going out every weekend and I didn't want you to think that I didn't want to see you, but I can't see you this weekend. I just wanted to let you know that ahead of time so you didn't feel like I was ignoring you." He made me feel like he actually thought about my feelings. And he knew me well enough to know that I was still a bit vulnerable still from my previous relationship.

I was so impressed by the way Lynne took care of Lakisha. I like to have fun and enjoy life, but people matter to me. I really respect people who care about other people and take care of them. I admire people who make sacrifices for the ones they care about. And Lynne definitely cared about Lakisha. It was easy for me to want to be with her and want to have a family. She was really special.

We didn't have a ring when I proposed but I decided to have dinner with Lynne's parents and Lynne. I wanted to do it with them so that we were all on the same page. Her parent's were old school and were uncomfortable with her being with a man out of wedlock. They obviously knew that she was an adult and a mom and everything else, but they were happy to know that we wanted to get married and have a family. So we had dinner and I asked her dad's permission.

But one other thing happened before that. One day Lakisha said to us, "Let's pretend that you're my dad and my mom's the mom and I'm the kid!" And Paul said, "Okay..." because we were just playing house. Then afterwards, when she went to bed, he said, "We have to figure out what we're doing because I don't want to disappoint Lakisha. We have to decide whether we're going to be dating like friends and then I won't be over here as much, or if we're going to be together and make a commitment to each other." And so we did!

Lynne let me know that she thought I might be a good dad. So that gave me the green light to go further. Lakisha and I spent a lot of time together because Lynne was still in school, so I read to her and played games. We played with her Care Bears and did this and that. One day while we were playing I told her that I was going to be her dad and I asked her what she thought about that.

And she said, "I'm not calling you daddy till after you marry my mom!"

She sure did, didn't she? And I said, "That's very good Lakisha. I'm okay with that."

Then after the wedding she walked right up to him, grabbed onto his leg, and said, "Hi, Daddy!"

That's right. That was the first time she said that.

She meant what she said. She was very organized and knew what the rules were. There were lots of rules in her little head.

After we got married, Lynne wanted to have another kid right away. But I didn't want to do that until she finished college.

He also really wanted to make sure that Lakisha felt like he was her dad. So we waited about five years before having another baby. Lakisha was nine. But I had a miscarriage before our son was born and that was very, very hard for me. It took us a long time to get pregnant, and to lose the baby four months in was devastating. But we got pregnant again right away and now we have a wonderful son. It was hard though. People would come up to Paul while I was pregnant and say things like, "Oh, it'll be so nice to have a child that's yours." And he would always say, "I already do."

From my perspective, many of the high points that we have had over the years involve our kids. And there's no dollar amount you can put on that. There are plenty of people who were doing other things while their kids were growing up and that's fine, they've accomplished a lot of stuff. But we were on the scene while our kids were doing things and we allowed them to have various options with lessons and stuff. And that was so satisfying. Maybe my job wasn't the greatest, but my kids were doing things that were really amazing. They were really spectacular things that I dreamed of doing when I was a kid. When Lakisha got her black belt in Tae Kwon Do, seeing her break the board and deal with these big guys was fantastic. And the connections we made over the years because of our kids were important in enriching our lives as well.

The connections we've made through our children and their activities has made our community bigger and our lives so much richer. But the good news is, when our son went off to college and we were finally all alone, we found out that we still like to do stuff together! That was a good thing to realize. Sometimes kids leave and people don't know what to do with themselves anymore. But we have a lot of little things we like to do together. We go for bike rides, we drink coffee and go to movies.

We travel together. We like walking around new towns and going to restaurants and meeting new people.

We're pretty easy going. We just like to explore.

I think at first, when love is young and everything is new and exciting, it's a little easier to overlook things about a person that might be harder to deal with. Over time, after you get married and go through hardships and have kids, you almost become kind of like business partners. You run a family together. You buy houses and cars and take care of all the bills. You have to be careful budgeting money. That has been a challenge over the years. But we sought help when we needed it. There were times in our relationship where we weren't communicating with each other, and that leads to really big problems. If you can't talk about money or other things going on in your relationship that aren't quite right, that can be big trouble. If you don't get help; a mediator, or somebody outside of the relationship to help you stay on track, that is what leads to a lot of people splitting up.

We always went to therapy when we needed to. And the good thing is that we were both open to that. Both of us believe therapy is helpful.

I know and see the value of therapy. A lot of times people personalize things and they just think that the other person is a jerk or whatever, but a lot of times it's just a problem with communication. And that can be helped. I think that's why Lynne and I are still able to feel so good about each other after all these years. We keep trying. When I look at her I still see the wonderful woman that I met many years ago.

I realize when I go out with my girlfriends that there's really no other person I want to spend my time with other than Paul. I like to go out with my girlfriends but I can't necessarily even say that I'd want to go on a long vacation with them. I guess I just feel comfortable with Paul. I can be myself. I don't hide too much, or anything really...that's probably a problem.

It's only natural to have a little mystery.

We only have one bathroom so there's not much mystery. We're working on the mystery part. But we've had lots of ups and downs and we just keep getting through them. When our kids have struggles, it's hard for us, but I think it only makes us stronger. We try to figure out how to help our kids together and try to give them the best we can give them. The good thing is, we agree on a lot of things. We agree on what's important in life. Even though we haven't gotten to go to a lot of places and do a lot of things, we don't feel like we need that in order to have a good life. We have a good life right here on our little street.

ABOUT THE AUTHOR

As a performer, Anna Bowen has toured the United States and Europe, working with legends such as Patti Labelle, Nile Rogers, Dionne Warwick, Tom Jones, Slash and Mickey Dolenz. She has been seen on television in *Law and Order, As The World Turns, Mixology,* and *Castle.* She can be seen around Los Angeles singing with the "Overstreets New Orleans Jazz Band," "The Melodies" and "Velvet Mood." This is her first book. More information can be found at **www.AnnaBowen.com**.

Printed in Great Britain
by Amazon